What people say
about *When Waters Stir* . . .

Rich and Lynette Scherber poured their hearts and souls into the cause of redeeming and loving desperate, broken, and addicted people. Their faithful leadership of MNTC resulted in countless lives being saved, restored, and redeemed. Their tireless work is a shining example of loving God and loving others.

Tim Pawlenty
Former Governor of the State of Minnesota

Blending purity of heart with resilience and a daily commitment to lighting a path for those who struggle with nearly insurmountable addiction, Rich and Lynette have created an exponentially lasting legacy of hope and transformational healing. Their unwavering dedication has channeled the flow of love with amazing results. Minnesota Adult and Teen Challenge and its clarity of purpose is possibly the best example of one couple's passion for living an authentic life of true compassion.

Mary Pawlenty
Minnesota District Court Judge (Ret.)

Rich and Lynette Scherber live a life of asking, seeking, and knocking at God's door. They see the treasure in jars of clay and spend their time in the work of redemption. Because of their commitment, not only has the greater Twin Cities area seen lives that were being lost now become lives of usefulness and purpose, but they have also created a model that other communities now mirror. This book is an inspiration to persevere through trial, to say yes when you are called and to remember that each life has value.

Char Johansen

Every year at our charity golf tournament for the last 15 years, I have made the following statement. Rich and Lynette are the best and most gifted people I have ever seen at what they do. We're lucky they're serving God and not in the furniture business because they would kick our butts.

Wayne Johansen
HOM Furniture Founding Family

Rich and Lynette are absolutely committed to helping the least fortunate among us as vehicles of God's grace. Whenever I am around the two of them, their passion and determination to assist this group is evident and entirely infectious. This memoir is a truly inspirational story of faith, redemption, and hope. Rich and Lynette's tireless efforts on behalf of people at the full depths of addiction and despair is, at its core, lifesaving. Rich's humble account of the joys and struggles of building Minnesota Adult and Teen Challenge is uplifting, enlightening, and the culmination of answered prayers.

Steve McDaniels
Midwest Motors Group

This book reflects both Pastor Rich's deep faith and God's consistent hand in steering the Minnesota Adult and Teen Challenge organization, transforming it from a battered, insolvent ministry into one of the state's largest and most well-respected drug and alcohol treatment organizations. On a personal note, it has been such a blessing to me to be part of this Christian organization for so many years.

Jay Coughlan
CEO, Coughlan Consulting

When Waters Stir is an incredible and humbling reflection of God's presence and Pastor Rich's faith, passion, and vision. It is a story of miracles, grit, tenacity, survival, endurance, and saving lives through Christ. A fast and inspiring read.

Jeannine M Rivet
President, K.A.H.R. Foundation

My wife Becky and I have had the pleasure of working with Minnesota Adult and Teen Challenge for many years. We have been exposed to the extraordinary stories of healing again and again. Each one is a miracle and evidence of God's hands on this ministry. Rich and Lynette's story is an amazing journey of faith and courage and one that will inspire all readers to listen and trust in things never imagined possible. Enjoy!

Paul Walser
Chairman of the 2021 National Automobile Dealers Association
Partner of the Walser Automotive Group

When
Waters
Stir

THE MIRACULOUS JOURNEY OF
MINNESOTA ADULT AND TEEN CHALLENGE

PASTOR RICH SCHERBER

Cover design and interior formatting by Anne McLaughlin,
Blue Lake Design • bluelakedesign.com

ISBN: 978-1-947505-40-7

First printing 2022
Published by Baxter Press, Friendswood, Texas
Printed in the United States of America

For an angel went down
at a certain time into the pool
and stirred up the water;
then whoever stepped in first,
after the stirring of the water,
was made well of whatever
disease he had.

John 5:4

Table of Contents

John 5:1–8

After this there was a feast of the Jews, and Jesus went up to Jerusalem. Now there is in Jerusalem by the Sheep Gate a pool, which is called in Hebrew, Bethesda, having five porches. In these lay a great multitude of sick people, blind, lame, paralyzed, waiting for the moving of the water. For an angel went down at a certain time into the pool and stirred up the water; then whoever stepped in first, after the stirring of the water, was made well of whatever disease he had. Now a certain man was there who had an infirmity thirty-eight years. When Jesus saw him lying there, and knew that he already had been in that condition a long time, He said to him, "Do you want to be made well?"

The sick man answered Him, "Sir, I have no man to put me into the pool when the water is stirred up; but while I am coming, another steps down before me."

Jesus said to him, "Rise, take up your bed and walk."

Preface

Dear Reader,

There is a passage in the Bible that often comes to mind when I recall the stories of how I have seen God move at Minnesota Adult and Teen Challenge. John 5:2-8 recounts how the healing waters of the pool at Bethesda would be stirred when God was ready to act. This story has often served as a metaphor for something that I have felt God doing, a stirring in my spirit when He was about to do the impossible. This book is a collection of stories about times when God stirred the waters, we took a step of faith, and God moved in miraculous ways to heal His people.

As you read this account, please keep in mind that quotes are my closest recollection of the exact words that were used, and some names may be excluded or changed to protect privacy. Also, the name of our organization is officially Minnesota Teen Challenge, but for several years, we have done business as Minnesota Adult and Teen Challenge. You will see these names and the abbreviation MNTC used interchangeably throughout the book.

This is my story, but it is also God's. I hope these stories stir your heart and encourage your faith like they have mine. You see, I've spent the past 30 years working with an organization that assists people struggling with life-controlling chemical addictions. But I also have my own addiction story. It started with alcohol in my elementary school years, and by the time I was fourteen, I was using drugs and alcohol on a regular basis. By my early twenties, they had consumed my life.

In 1972, while on my way to sell and deliver drugs to a group of young people in the community of Buffalo, Minnesota, I encountered the message of the Gospel for the first time in my life. A group of local Christians who were concerned with the growing drug problem in the community had launched a street outreach to area kids. They targeted an area called Wide Street where hundreds of kids congregated each night during the summer months.

Earlier that day I had picked up half a kilo of marijuana and a large bag of pills with plans to sell them in Buffalo that evening. As I approached Wide Street, I noticed about 75 to 100 youths had already gathered. The plan was to pick up several kegs of beer, along with the drugs, and we would all go out to a party. Because I had a large quantity of illegal substances in my vehicle, and the Wright County Police had arrested me previous times, I was nervous as I waited for our contacts to arrive. It was then that several Christians who were involved in the street outreach approached my group and began sharing the Gospel message. Everyone else seemed to ignore them, but for some reason I listened to every word they spoke.

You see, in previous months, addiction to drugs and the crazy lifestyle associated with it had all caught up with me. I was just sick and tired of being sick and tired to the point where I had attempted suicide numerous times. After hearing the Good News of the Gospel that night, I was given an invitation that would forever change the course of my personal history. I accepted Jesus Christ into my life as my Lord and Savior, right there in front of my jeering friends. "Hey, look! The Jesus freaks got Scherber!" But I could not have cared less. I had found something real.

The conversion was so instantaneous and dramatic that the next day I gathered all of my drugs and drug paraphernalia, heaped them into a pile, and after "baptizing" it with gasoline, threw a burning match. What freedom I felt! I grabbed a large knife, marched back into a secluded field, and cut down several dozen marijuana plants that I had been cultivating. It was over. I had burned the bridges to my drug lifestyle. The spiritual growth that took place in my life over the next few years was proof of this.

In 1974, I entered full-time ministry. My first assignment was to travel with a street ministry primarily reaching out to Native Americans, Mexican migrating laborers, and people living in parks and drug-infested inner cities. In 1976, I married Lynette and went back to school to acquire a bachelor's in theology and later a master's in psychology and counseling. While working on my degrees, I was a senior pastor in northern Minnesota for seven years.

From 1984 to 1991, Lynette and I served as missionaries to Africa. We were assigned to work in the segregated townships of South Africa during the height of apartheid. From neglect and desperation, they had become very dangerous places by the time we arrived. The South African police would ride through the streets in armored vehicles holding assault rifles. During these years, I experienced dozens of violent riots where my life was at risk. Many evenings I would return home with broken windows in my vehicle, describing the narrow escape to my wife. Despite the constant danger, God gave me great success. I was able to build nine large church buildings (even making the cement blocks by hand), hold hundreds of large outdoor crusades where tens of thousands of decisions were made for Christ, establish new churches, and help strengthen and support our existing congregations.

It was during our first visit back to the states that the story of Minnesota Teen Challenge (MNTC) begins. Needless to say, we were tired and looking forward to a season of rest and relaxation. But as you will soon read, the Lord had something quite different planned for the Scherber family...

The Scherber family's return from South Africa in late 1990

Rich holding a Kirby vacuum similar to the one
he inherited in 1991

1

A Used Kirby

As the landing gear screeched on the tarmac, touching down on American soil, a rush of emotions engulfed me. It was late summer 1990 when we returned from the violent civil unrest in South Africa having served five years as foreign missionaries in the segregated townships. I cannot begin to describe the overwhelming anticipation of reuniting with our family and friends, shadowed by the gnawing concern for struggling congregations and new converts we had left behind. But we were home now, a year of visiting supporting churches in front of us. As we stepped off the plane, we naïvely expected to find things as we had left them those several years earlier. But instead, we found ourselves facing our brave new world like deer staring into headlights.

Once familiar adults and children had aged noticeably, and daily life had changed in a thousand big and small ways. Soda machines talked, vans had extended front ends, rap music filled the air, and the Cold War was over. We were suddenly and unexpectedly foreigners again–this time in our own country and among our own people. Despite this, we were eagerly looking forward to the embraces of our loved ones and finding some much-needed "R and R," as indeed our vacation was long overdue.

But instead of catching our breath, we barely had time to say 'hello' before pastors who'd heard we were back in the states began contacting us. Because most churches have their missions conventions in the fall, our speaking schedules quickly filled up. From day one—living out of suitcases that we'd packed in South Africa—we started traveling across the country. I remember this transition being a huge step for our now elementary-age daughters who remembered life only in South Africa. America was a much different place for them. Most of our belongings being on the other side of the world, and calling a tiny, rented apartment 'home' made things even more challenging. Today, I have a good deal of compassion for missionaries who find themselves in this same situation.

Months of traveling long distances for both midweek and weekend services began to take its toll on Lynette and the girls. It was not uncommon for us to leave on a Saturday, drive hundreds of miles, have morning and evening services (sometimes hours apart), and then drive all the way back so the girls could attend school the next morning. We did this for nearly a year without a break.

After several months at this pace, we were invited to drive to Missouri and meet with our missions leadership to talk about future opportunities. They were all aware of the increasing violence where we had been working and were concerned for our welfare. As we met with them, they praised our accomplishments and talked about several opportunities throughout the southern region of Africa. And since our ministry as church builders and evangelists had been so fruitful, several regional African leaders had contacted them to request our help. One exciting opportunity that was presented to us was in the country of Mozambique. This country in southern Africa had just ended a civil war, and Christian churches were struggling greatly. Another opportunity was for us to return to South Africa. When we first accepted our assignment there five years earlier, we were sent to the most remote and austere region—the desert of the Orange Free State. However, we were now receiving an open invitation to serve anywhere in the country.

They were all aware of the increasing violence where we had been working and were concerned for our welfare.

Years earlier, I had driven through several of the large townships near Johannesburg, like Soweto, and I had been moved to tears by the great need—longing to be located there. And now, not just one, but several open doors of ministry suddenly lay ahead of us. We were not sure of the future, but Lynette and I could sense that God was doing something new.

Toward the end of our year-long itineration, several other opportunities also developed. One that really caught our attention was an offer to be considered for the senior pastorate of a large church in Wisconsin. They had been longtime supporters of our ministry, and we knew the church well. This was a healthy congregation in a good community with precious people who loved us. When Lynette and I met with their leadership and they began to share about the opportunities of ministry, we quickly realized that if we were going to be staying in the states, this would be the perfect scenario.

There was a Christian school on site for our girls to attend, the salary was nearly twice what we were currently earning as missionaries, they were solid financially with a beautiful building, and there was an open position for the minister of music (my wife has a master's degree in music). This opportunity and the timing of it was almost too good to be true! I remember leaving the interview bewildered. Could God be in this? At the same time, our Minnesota district leadership presented to us some home missions opportunities. The thought of settling down in one place, not having to live out of a suitcase, not having to say goodbye to our family for another four years, and no longer struggling with meager finances sounded very attractive to say the least. On top of that, throw in the fatigue we were experiencing! A long rest with a less stressful lifestyle was quite compelling indeed.

As we were nearing the completion of our furlough in the states, our missions leadership contacted us again to talk about finalizing our plans for ministry in Africa. They needed our decision so they could plan. They also shared with us that the general superintendent for the entire South African denomination had recently contacted them. He especially requested that our family come back to South Africa to assist them and said pointedly that our ministry was needed 'very badly'!

Lynette and I asked for just a few extra days to seek God's direction. I remember this being a very difficult time–actually, one of the harder times in my life. We were being pressured for an answer, but I simply couldn't give them one.

As we weighed what we thought was our final decision, I received an evening phone call from our state superintendent. He wanted to know if Lynette and I could join him for breakfast early the next morning. The plan was to first meet at a certain church in downtown Minneapolis and go to breakfast from there. I was unsure exactly what he wanted to talk about, but I expected it involved our plans (and budget) for the future.

The next morning, Lynette and I arrived on the doorsteps of a run-down inner-city church. I had never been at this church before and knew very little about it. The foyer of the building looked disheveled and in disarray, and I noticed a distinct rank odor. I also noticed a group of seven men sitting around a table having some sort of meeting. One of the individuals was our superintendent.

"Rich and Lynette, come join us. We have been waiting for you."

I commented, "What is this? I thought we were going to breakfast."

He then said, "We'll have breakfast later. This is the MNTC Board. They want to talk to you." I recognized about half of the men at the table—pastors of local churches from the area. After the introductions, one of them asked us if we knew anything about MNTC. I told him I knew about the ministry of David Wilkerson and Teen Challenge from the book, *The Cross and the Switchblade*. I said that I was also aware that they were trying to start a program in St. Paul shortly before we left for South Africa six years earlier.

"We did get a program started in St. Paul, but it was quickly shut down. We haven't had a residential program since then, and that was years ago," one of the men sadly said, and I sensed a tense atmosphere in the room. I was about to find out why.

Someone handed us a newspaper and pointed toward an article on the front page that read, 'Two Women Sue Minister, Charge That He Sexually Exploited Them'. The article went on to talk about a local minister who was being sued by multiple women in his congregation who had been taken advantage of during counseling and ministry times. When we finished reading the article, someone with a broken voice said, "This is our Teen Challenge director, and since this article has come out, other women also have stepped forward with similar allegations."

They estimated that this could lead to a million-dollar lawsuit, and MNTC did not have proper insurance to cover this. They explained to me that the MNTC director was also the pastor of the very church in which we were now meeting.

I asked about the home that they had started in St. Paul years ago. I was told that it was sold, and all the assets from the sale of the home were gone. The ministry itself was expected to be in great debt. I would find out later that the outstanding balance exceeded $30,000. With my mind spinning, I asked if there was anything at all left of the ministry. The response is one I will never forget. "We do have a used Kirby vacuum cleaner." Back then, a new Kirby sold for about $1500. And although it was a valuable item, the ministry was bankrupt and everyone knew it.

However, one item that was missed during the inventory conversation was the MNTC telephone. During our 20-minute visit with the board, that old greasy analog phone must have rung a dozen times, and each time it would ring 10, 15, and even 20 times before silencing only briefly. Finally, Lynette couldn't hold back any longer and asked if someone needed to answer the phone. It sounded like someone was desperate to be calling so incessantly.

The response is one I will never forget. "We do have a used Kirby vacuum cleaner."

One man replied, "There's no one on staff to pick up that phone. I try to when I can make the time, but it just keeps ringing. That's the only thing left of this ministry–the live MNTC phone line." I saw Lynette swallow hard.

Finally, I asked the question, "What does this have to do with us? We thought we were going to breakfast."

"The board wants to know if you would be interested in taking over the ministry?" At that, I began a barrage of questions, beginning with clarity on the church. The congregation was only a few years old. It had been a congregation of about 500 people, but since the media reports on the pastor's alleged misconduct, attendance had dropped dramatically. The church had a huge mortgage, and many suburbanites who had joined to help with the mission financially were now disgruntled and leaving.

Taken aback by the whole sequence of events, I said something along the lines of, "Let me get this right. The individual involved in this alleged sexual misconduct is the MNTC director and pastor of this church. Both ministries are working together. This scandal is making the newspaper headlines. You're telling me that now multiple other women, on top of those mentioned in the newspaper, have come forward with similar allegations and will probably be joining in the lawsuit? Regrettably, MNTC has no insurance to cover these claims, and they will probably be named in the lawsuit? And now the church has dwindled down to almost nothing, with massive indebtedness, and many of the sub-urbanite families—the tithers—have left or will be leaving? And as if things couldn't get worse, MNTC also has massive debt with its only asset being a *used* vacuum cleaner? Am I understanding this all correctly?"

I don't know what your reaction would have been, but I found this whole scenario most disturbing. How could things have gotten so bad? I think everyone at that table was asking themselves the same question. I said something like, "You're inviting me to accept the leadership? What an honor." At this, nervous laughter erupted around the room, with heads shaking in disbelief that all this had just happened.

My attention was drawn to one man, tears welling in his eyes, who seemed unaffected by the absurdity of the moment. Things quickly quieted down as all attention focused on him. Gathering his composure he shared, "We are all devastated! This church and MNTC are in shambles! However, this is a missions church—full of hurting people. Both this church and Teen Challenge need to stay alive. I have served alongside this ministry and have been answering that MNTC phone when I am able, and I have been talking to some of the most desperate human beings I have ever spoken to in my life. Rich, I know who you are! You came from addiction, you have a master's in psychology and counseling, your whole ministry has been with this population, and look what you did in Africa! You are perfect for the job. We need you! I'm going to ask one favor. Would you at least pray about this and ask the Lord what He wants you to do?" Lynette and I both nodded.

The board had other business to discuss, so we excused ourselves and told the superintendent that we would go out to breakfast another time.

Even though we probably weren't in that meeting for more than half an hour, throughout the day I couldn't stop thinking about it. What a strange meeting it was! Every night of our 45 years of marriage, Lynette and I have our prayer time together before going to sleep. That night we again prayed for our kids, our family, and for direction in our lives. I kissed her goodnight and went to sleep. For some reason, I woke up around 3:00 in the morning. I heard Lynette roll over a few times. "Lynette, are you awake?"

"Rich, I never went to sleep. I keep hearing that phone ringing—over and over—with no one to answer it. On the other end of that line are desperate people. They could be our own daughters, or relatives, or neighbors. They ARE somebody's loved ones. I am so burdened. I don't know if the Lord has laid this on my heart or if I am just saddened by the situation. If it is the Lord, is it possible that He could be calling us to this ministry? Someone needs to pick up that phone."

I was wide awake by now! I said, "Lynette, if we come off the mission field, we may lose most of our support."

She replied, "We don't know if He is calling us to MNTC, but could we pray that He calls someone? The need is so great! But if by some chance He is calling us, He would make a way. If our support is dropped, maybe I could get a job teaching to support our family so you could take over the ministry." We prayed for God's guidance, for Him to send someone to pick up the MNTC phone, and then we both went to sleep.

Missions church where Teen Challenge housed its offices and where Rich filled in as pastor

Local park outreach with missions church

2

Answering the Call

Lynette and I didn't make any decisions the next day, but we did agree to make this a matter of serious prayer. It was only a few days later that I received a call from one of the elders of the inner-city church. He explained that he knew of our recent MNTC board meeting and asked if I would be willing to come and fill in a few Sundays until they could find a replacement pastor. We still badly needed some rest, but since I was just finishing my African itineration, I agreed to begin the following Sunday.

When our family arrived for the service, we found a mixed congregation ranging from suburbanites who had a sincere desire to help the needy, to the homeless and those living in shelters. What do you say to a congregation like this? Because of the open wounds of such a diverse group of people, it was hard to know where to begin. And to further complicate the situation, our welcome also appeared to be mixed! Evidently, some churchgoers were angry that the church leaders had asked the pastor to step down, and the fact that the same leadership asked me to step in and help showed that I was not "trustworthy" either. Fortunately though, there were others who were happy that someone was willing to help hold the church together until things could stabilize.

Setting the mixed reactions aside, my attention was drawn to the dozens of hurting people who had come in from the local shelters and off the streets. Each Sunday, a meal was provided after the service, and people often came by the hundreds.

That morning, I preached and gave the invitation for prayer, and the altars were full. After the service, the girls, Lynette, and I went downstairs to assist those serving the meal. As the crowd came through the food line, you could smell the stench of alcohol on many of them and scores of others were high on drugs. It seemed like the majority of those who came that morning were chronic substance abusers.

"These same people come week after week," one of the food service workers told me. "Some come just for the meal, but others come early for the services. They are generally the first people to respond to the altar call for prayer. Nothing ever changes. Each week they come back in the same condition. They are bound by the drugs and alcohol and can't seem to break the addiction."

Then a different worker chimed in, "We keep hoping that MNTC will start a residential program in this city, but nothing has ever happened. These people need long-term, Christ-centered help. Please Pastor Rich, maybe you can help us."

This comment really hit home. I think this was, ultimately, one of the major turning points in my decision to take over the MNTC program. It moved me because I also came out of years of addiction, and I knew exactly what many of these folks were going through. There is nothing worse than the hopelessness of being trapped and finding yourself powerless to escape.

On the way home from church that Sunday, our family talked about what we had just experienced. We were all so very moved. Thank God that our girls have grown up around missions all their lives. We had just witnessed that *"missions"* doesn't only mean Africa.

Not having a senior pastor around presented a lot of problems. On top of this, there were the legal, financial, and damage-control issues related to the previous pastor departing. As you can guess, my one-day-visit turned into a daily request for help. It really was overwhelming.

MNTC was falling further into debt, and the threat of the ministry collapsing became stronger. It needed someone's full attention. The church, however, didn't need any more surprises! I was very concerned that without a strong leader to take my place, the church wouldn't survive. They were touching hundreds of homeless and transient people daily, and this mission *had* to continue. To be honest, not taking on the pastorate was a tough decision to make at the time. If I am called to missions, pastoring this church would certainly fulfill that call. Why would I leave this to go start a ministry where there was nothing but a bad reputation and debt? But whenever I asked God for an answer, I always felt that tugging back to MNTC.

All of this was happening during the same time that our African missions organization was waiting for our answer. People have asked over the years, "Why did you and Lynette ultimately decide not to return to Africa?" Looking back, I think there were a combination of factors that impacted our decision. While it was true that the South African townships were becoming increasingly dangerous and living out of a suitcase was becoming old hat, far more pressing was an unshakeable nudge towards MNTC. I kept going back to the conversation Lynette and I had months earlier in the middle of the night. *"Rich, I think we need to pray about this Teen Challenge Ministry."*

Lynette grew up in a strong Christian family. She has faithfully served the Lord all her life. God has given her a unique gift. I know her well enough to know that when God is speaking to her with such great passion, it's good to listen. Also, the more we prayed together, the stronger I felt the tug of God on my heart for the MNTC ministry. I knew there would be a lot of challenges, but I also knew He would provide. God had done so many great miracles during our missionary stay in South Africa. He surely wasn't going to fail us now.

Personally, Teen Challenge has always been near to my heart. In the 1970's, I followed the ministry of David Wilkerson, watched *The Cross and Switchblade* movie, and read many of his books. Over the years, I've visited several Teen Challenge programs across the country and have always respected his work. Most of my own previous ministry included helping those stuck in addiction, even when serving overseas. I identify with them! I was intrigued with the idea of taking over MNTC, even though it was in dreadful shape. However, the idea of taking over the church at the same time, especially with both ministries being in massive debt, scared me. I knew I couldn't do them both justice. The ministries needed their own sovereignty.

As I look back, I remember this period being a time of great soul-searching for us. I had definitely felt God's call to overseas missions. In fact, I remember the first serious conversation I ever had with Lynette. I needed to make sure that whoever would be my life partner would also have the same calling. Were we now disobeying God? Does God place you in one place only, or does He move people into various roles and assign new duties within a broader sphere of ministry? While this dilemma weighed constantly on our minds, the live Teen Challenge phone line continued to beckon us like a Macedonian call.

We finally took the leap of faith. After making the decision not to return to Africa, our next step would be to contact the MNTC Board Chairman to let him know, followed by the Foreign Missions Department. The first conversation was received with joyous relief. The board chairman was a dear minister with previous experience with Teen Challenge in New York and was now pastoring a small Latino congregation in St. Paul. I could tell that the media coverage of the former MNTC Director's behavior, the potential lawsuits, and the financial pressures from the ministry's debt were all starting to take their toll on him.

When I made the call to tell him that God had spoken to our hearts to take over the ministry, I sensed that he had an urgency to pass the baton to me as soon as possible. His only further encouragement was to not try and pastor the church and develop the MNTC ministry at the same time. He made it clear that both ministries would suffer. I communicated to him that we agreed and were only willing to help at the church until a replacement could be found.

When the church congregation heard that we would be taking over MNTC, many were elated. Remember, in most of their minds, the church and Teen Challenge were one. Some even referred to it as the "Teen Challenge Church." Fortunately, MNTC had acquired its own 501c3 nonprofit status four years before the church had even started, but this information was not generally known. What most people didn't realize was the fact that MNTC was literally no more than a phone in an office–a phone that rang incessantly with individuals needing treatment. And since MNTC had no counselors, no therapists, and no program, individuals needing help were referred out to other Teen Challenge residential programs across the country.

The second call, to the foreign mission's department, was not as joy filled. We'd had a very successful ministry in Africa, building nine churches and witnessing literally tens of thousands come to Christ. All of this took place during some of the most dangerous and turbulent days in South Africa's history. Our missions leadership had great hopes that we would continue our work throughout the southern region of Africa. Hearing our decision to leave was not welcomed news. To be honest, we felt some shame, disdain, and scorn from a lot of the Christian community. Many of our supporting churches dropped our support immediately. Some thought we were staying in the United States for an easy way out. If people only knew, South African missions would be a cakewalk compared to what we would go through in the next few months. We would be jumping out of the frying pan and into a blazing fire.

Hearing our decision to leave was not welcomed news. To be honest, we felt some shame, disdain, and scorn from a lot of the Christian community.

3

Have We Hit Bottom Yet?

A month or so after taking on the MNTC leadership position, I was finally able to calculate the ministry's outstanding financial obligations. They, I mean WE, were indebted more than $30,000. I had also heard back from several ministry supporters who, as I had suspected, were frustrated with the recent turn of events involving the previous leader and had decided to drop our support. To make matters worse, even though I was filling in at the church (without any compensation), their board met with me and asked if MNTC would now start paying rent. I was told that the church needed the space (it was an old creaky-floored room with a lightbulb suspended from the ceiling and a sticky wooden desk), and if we couldn't pay rent, we would have to locate elsewhere. It looked like we were being pressed in from all sides. So now we would have no offices, huge indebtedness, potential lawsuits, no assets, a dreadful reputation, and much of my foreign mission's support had just dried up. I thank God that a few of our supporting churches stood with us during this time.

I was convinced we'd hit bottom until I heard the rumors of the MNTC Board's discussions on expansion. They had neglected to inform me that the ministry was currently in the process of taking out a mortgage to purchase a property in Ortonville, Minnesota with plans to create a new men's residential program for the state. Ortonville is a small farming town of 1800 people located more than 170 miles straight west of Minneapolis. It sits right on the South Dakota border, just a few miles down the road from Brookings Teen Challenge (the only Teen Challenge center in South Dakota). I was floored.

Why in the world would anyone want to start a major program so close to another existing center, and take out a mortgage which would result in debt on top of existing debt? Even more, why would anyone want to be hundreds of miles away from major population centers? Where would we ever find the staff? The whole concept was absurd.

As I asked around, I found out that apparently this wasn't the first ill-advised move the ministry had made. Years earlier, MNTC had purchased a building in St. Paul for a women's center. Unfortunately, the leadership didn't realize that you can't just buy a facility anywhere, in any neighborhood, and then open up a group home without consulting the city zoning administrators or following city zoning codes. Because the center did not have proper licensing, the City of St. Paul shut down the program just months after it opened.

Unfortunately, the donors who had sacrificed to help purchase this building watched helplessly as it was closed, and their donations quickly vanished.

As soon as I heard the history of the St. Paul project and found out more about the board's plans to move forward with Ortonville, I set up a meeting with the chairman. I communicated my concerns and laid out an ultimatum. I would not be moving my family to Ortonville to run a program, and if he wanted me to continue to be their director, our first order of business would be to get out of debt, not accumulate more. After some discussion he agreed, and the plans for Ortonville were tabled. I believe we caught this just in the nick of time as the board was only months away from closing on the property. Ortonville would have been a huge mistake for the ministry. I'm not sure MNTC would have survived another catastrophe.

For four or five months we were overwhelmed taking care of the church while Teen Challenge sat on the back burner, when one day out of nowhere, I received a call from the MNTC Board Chairman. He told me the most unusual story. He said that he had been at a café earlier that morning, and he had met a stranger who said he would like to donate a large four-plex apartment building to MNTC. The facility had easy access to the freeway, would hold up to 20 clients, and we could have it for free. He told me, "Rich, I think this is it. The guy wants us to come see the property right away. I unfortunately can't make it, but you take care of this. Let him know that we want to take it."

The chairman gave me the donor's phone number, and I made the call. The conversation was short and to the point. He wanted me to meet him at 3021 Clinton Avenue in an hour, and he would show me the property. I was expecting to hear more details about the building and why the donor was motivated to give such a huge contribution. Maybe he had heard about our need through one of the supporting churches or had a loved one who had been helped through a Teen Challenge program elsewhere. Regardless, I couldn't wait to call Lynette and give her the good news.

Because I didn't know South Minneapolis that well, I didn't recognize the address. I dug out my old map and found directions. As I drove down Lake Street approaching Clinton Avenue, I noticed a large pornographic bookstore located just a short distance away. On the sidewalk were a number of scantily dressed women trying to attract attention from the traffic going by. I would find out later that this area was a center for prostitution, and Clinton Avenue was one of the most drug-riddled areas in the city. The street where this house was located was commonly known as "Crack Alley."

The street where this house was located was commonly known as "Crack Alley."

As I turned the corner and entered Clinton Avenue, I saw several condemned buildings along the street. Just two houses down was 3021. I could see that the windows were boarded up and the building was in shambles. I drove up and got out of the car. A man approached me carrying a clipboard. We greeted, and he then began to give me a brief history of the property. He recapped his meeting with our board chairman earlier that morning in a local café. He was looking for a nonprofit organization he could donate the property to so he could benefit from the tax write-off. I asked if he knew anything about MNTC, and he told me that he had never heard about us before that morning.

He handed me a purchase agreement, and said, "I talked this over with your board chairman, and he said you guys will take it. Sign here." I remember telling him that I needed to wait and talk to the other leaders, but he was very insistent that if we wanted the property, we had to take it on the spot. He said, "You are taking the property as is, but I promise you there are no back taxes or liens." He said he would put this in writing. There were no cell phones back then to call anyone, so I had to trust that the chairman had done his homework on the transaction. He said one last time that if I wanted it, I would have to take it now, or he would donate it to someone else. Hesitantly, I signed the document. He took his copy and quickly left.

Looking back now, I ask myself, "What were you thinking?" I should have just walked away saying, 'Thanks, but no thanks!' However, we were in a very desperate place. MNTC had nothing but debt, and this could get us started. Maybe this is what we'd needed all along. I hate debt, and the idea of going out and mortgaging a building to open a new MNTC center was clearly not an option. Now, 30 years later, with 13 residential programs across the state, and MNTC having grown to be one of the largest treatment providers in the Midwest, I am happy to say that we have never taken out a mortgage or allowed the ministry to go into debt.

Because my entire conversation with the donor took place on the sidewalk, once he left, I decided to take a look at our new "investment." Walking up to the main entrance, I noticed a *City of Minneapolis Condemnation Notice* attached to the front door. The doors were locked, and I had no keys, so I was unable to get inside. I decided to come back at a later time. So, I went home and called the board chairman to give him the update. He was thrilled with the news and very glad I had signed the purchase agreement so that we didn't lose the property. I shared his joy over the phone, but deep down I had an unsettled rumbling going on in my spirit.

That rumbling was well founded. This decrepit building became one of the greatest trials of my life. It brought me down to bedrock in my faith.

This decrepit building became one
of the greatest trials of my life.
It brought me down to bedrock
in my faith.

Clinton property condemned by the City of Minneapolis

The very room that you will read about in chapter 6
where Rich gives up

4

A Ray of Sunshine
(Through the Ceiling)

A few days after signing the purchase agreement, I was able to coordinate a preliminary inspection with the City of Minneapolis Building Inspection Department. Luckily, before we took over the property, I had checked with the city about zoning requirements and found that if we used the facility as a non-licensed Christian residence, and then used a local church for classes and programming, we would not have any issues with either licensing or zoning. We didn't want a repeat of the predicament the organization had been through with the St. Paul women's residence.

I'll never forget the day I met the inspector at the property. I had brought a whole box full of larger tools that I thought would be necessary for us to make our way into the building. When the inspector watched me pulling them out of my car he yelled, "You're probably not going to need those." I followed him along the narrow side of the house and watched him reach down into the bushes and pull out an old rotten ladder. He hoisted it under the plywood-covered window, and to my surprise, the plywood swung open, and he climbed inside. I followed as he informed me that this was an active crack house. The city knew this place well because the Minneapolis Police had raided it numerous times for drug use and prostitution. He turned on his flashlight, "Is anyone here?" he called loudly, searching rooms to make sure no one was hiding. Apparently, this was a routine procedure for him.

When he was confident the building was vacant, he suggested we start at the top and work our way downstairs. Sadly, in my wildest imagination, I could not have envisioned what this building looked and smelled like. It had been condemned for years with all the utilities turned off—no heat, water, electricity—nothing! And yet the facility *had* been occupied. The floors, walls, and fixtures of the bathrooms reeked of urine and feces. Mold was growing on the walls, and there were dirty mattresses on the floor in many of the rooms. Dirt and garbage were everywhere, and signs of drug use were evident. I didn't see any rats or mice during the inspection, but we sure saw our share of them during construction.

The inspector was very professional. As we reached the top floor, I saw that the roof had been leaking for a long time. Portions of the ceiling had collapsed, and there was at least one place where you could actually see light coming through. We were walking on hardwood floors that were bending up inches in every direction because of the moisture. The inspector grabbed his clipboard and began to speak as he wrote. "The first thing you will need to do is fix this roof." He further instructed that we would need to tear off most of the roof boards and planking. Better yet, the whole roof would need to come off and be replaced. For over an hour we went from one project to another that needed to be replaced, not repaired.

Portions of the ceiling had collapsed, and there was at least one place where you could actually see light coming through.

Because the renovations were so extensive, I will highlight just some of the bigger projects. After the roof, he turned his focus to the floors. He told me that the leaky roof had warped most of the hardwood, and he was expecting that the floorboards and joists were rotted as well. He was right! He then showed me the decaying windows overlaid with lead-based paint. He crushed some of the wood between his fingers and told me that all windows would need to be replaced. Any lead-based paint would also have to go. From there we went into the filthy bathrooms. He told me that we would need all new fixtures, and that all corroded metal water pipes would need to be replaced with copper pipes. He pointed to the broken walls and began to explain that all plaster would need to be removed because all the electrical in the entire four-plex must be replaced inside the walls. Room by room we worked our way down until we came to the basement. He pointed to the old gravity stove with the asbestos piping and said, "This all needs to go. There are no hot water lines or forced air vents in this complex for your heating. They will all be required and will have to be installed new." There was no good news; from top to bottom the place was a disaster.

When we were all done, he said, "Mr. Scherber, you don't want this four-plex. Do you understand that when the City of Minneapolis condemns a property, the new owners need to bring it back to current new construction standards? Some of the modifications that need to be done are almost impossible with this old construction layout."

Because this was my first visit inside the property, there was no way I could have anticipated discovering such deplorable conditions. I don't remember how I responded, but I do remember telling him that there is very little I could do at this point. The purchase agreement had been signed. "The building is ours, and now we have to deal with it." I thanked him for his time and got into my car feeling shaken.

On top of all of this, we still hadn't found a replacement pastor for the church. Despite the challenges of ministry in war-torn South Africa, this scenario was much more difficult. I left the Clinton property deeply discouraged that day. I remembered seeing candles laying around when walking through the building with the inspector. I was secretly hoping that by chance one of the squatters would forget to blow out one of those candles, and the building would burn to the ground. Fortunately, that never happened. God had better plans!

5

What If?

It would be six months before I went back to the Clinton property again. The pressures of both managing the inner-city church with their various outreach ministries, plus fundraising to keep MNTC alive, was far more than a full-time job. At last, the church was able to find a permanent pastor, and I was able to move on, or so I thought. It actually resulted in a delay of several more months before the new candidate was able to leave his present church and transition into this new role. In all, I ended up serving more than a year as pastor before I was released to fully focus my efforts on MNTC. And as I said before, there had been no payroll for the assignment. My wife had secured a teaching job, and for the most part, supported both our family and the ministry on her modest salary.

Because the offices for MNTC were still located at the church, I was being pulled away for other non-MNTC projects every time I came through the door. I quickly realized that my first order of business had to be moving the MNTC offices out of the church building. Not only was I being distracted by the business of the church, but our office itself was a complete disaster. Plaster was falling off the ceiling in several places, the carpet was putrid and torn, and the room hadn't been painted in decades. Plus, the church was now insisting that we start paying rent for that tiny space. Fortunately, our local denomination headquarters was only blocks away and heard about our plight. They had a few empty office spaces in their basement and offered them to us for a very nominal cost. Looking back, this was one of the best business decisions the ministry ever made.

Once distanced from the church, MNTC could now become my focus. My next two priorities were to dig the ministry out of debt and to begin tackling the Clinton property. I started by calling most of the churches that supported our ministry while we were in Africa. If you remember, in an earlier chapter I mentioned that many of our supporting churches dropped us immediately when we decided not to return overseas. I had hoped, since our focus was now on building a strong Teen Challenge ministry here in Minnesota, that local churches would joyfully renew their pledges. Unfortunately, this often was not the case. Because the MNTC ministry had struggled for 10 years with multiple directors leaving, a failed women's center in St. Paul, allegations of moral failure covered by the media, a tarnished reputation with no fruit, and multiple active lawsuits, many pastors I spoke with were reluctant to become involved.

It was most disheartening to hear this same sentiment echoed repeatedly phone call after phone call. They apologized for the bad news but said that, although their churches had been contributors in the past, in light of the rumors currently floating around about MNTC, they had decided to just move on. Some said that they had already transferred their support to the other similar ministries. Some even questioned why I would want to move ahead with MNTC when it was in such terrible shape, and since Minnesota had such good organizations already doing the work.

To be completely honest, I began asking myself this same question. Maybe Minnesota has enough Christian organizations across the state to care for the addiction community. Looking back now over the past 30 years and more than 20,000 individuals who have entered our program, I can see that obviously the enemy was working overtime to try and discourage me. But it wasn't so easy to see it then.

By this time the odds were stacked so high against me that things couldn't possibly get any worse. However, like clockwork, the next wave of discouragement came when I visited the City of Minneapolis Planning Department. The city planners told me that because the Clinton property was condemned, I would need to include with the permit a complete set of architectural drawings showing all remodeling construction. They also wanted specific plans relating to the new heating, electrical, and plumbing that would be installed. Right away, I cringed. I knew that architect fees average about 10 to 20 percent of the total cost on a project. This would be tens of thousands of dollars! The inspector did give me permission to pull a demo permit, however. This was good news since at least we could start the project.

Over the years, I have had several people tell me that God has granted me great tenacity and endurance. Webster's defines endurance as, "the ability to continue under pain and distress without resistance, or without being overcome." Tackling a total remodel on a project like this, without any financial capital, stretches the imagination of the words endurance and tenacity. This project would ultimately be one of the hardest things I have ever undertaken in my life. MNTC had virtually nothing except debt with multiple lingering lawsuits hanging over our heads. We didn't know the amounts, but were warned that in total, the lawsuits could potentially reach over a million dollars.

Then there were my own fears that I had to master. The greatest fears came in the form of "what if's." *What if* we finally were able to rehab the Clinton property, will the lawsuits end up taking it away? Was it even worth starting the project if potentially we could lose it all in the end? *What if* we can't raise the money to finish the project, and we end up with more debt? Who would be responsible? *What if* someone gets hurt during construction? How would we pay the medical bills? *What if* zoning doesn't give us the right permissions to use the facility as we want? During the next year, as I spent long hours laboring on this rehab, the "what if's" haunted me relentlessly. In a perfect world, perhaps MNTC would have avoided all these obstacles. Someone could have just given MNTC a multimillion-dollar donation. Then we could have purchased the perfect property with cash. We could have hired the right staff, purchased the right equipment, acquired the right vehicles, and designed a program that we all would be proud of. Unfortunately, there was no such donor. The early days of MNTC were all about survival.

The greatest fears came in the
form of "what if's."

Many long, lonely days and huge discouragements often came through the mailbox in the form of "canceling of support" letters. We had been back in the states for two and a half years by this time. There had been 12 months spent visiting supporting churches and another year filling in at the inner-city church. Now, 10 to 12 months of looming renovation on an old, condemned house lay ahead of me. That would end up being more than three years of exhausting work without any fruit to show for it. Add to this the ill-fated history of MNTC, and why would anyone want to continue their support?

However, there was a ray of hope I will never forget—while looking through the list of donors, I noticed a family that had recently sent in a generous gift. I recall that during one of my first visits with him, I shared some of my discouragement. "Reggie," I said, "I can't do this alone! I need your help! If you bail, I bail." And I meant it! It had come to the point where I felt utterly trapped and couldn't handle another discouragement. Reggie looked at me with tears in his eyes and told me we could count on him and Catherine. I didn't know this at the time, but despite personal financial difficulty they were facing, Catherine had encouraged Reggie to look into supporting our ministry. It was their generosity and faithfulness that literally kept this ministry alive. Graciously, God has blessed their faithfulness so that today Reggie's business has flourished into one of the largest property management companies in Minnesota. Even now, Reggie and Catherine Gassen still stand as some of our strongest supporters and two of my biggest heroes.

Rich with Pastor Ronnie Williams

John and Carol Koepcke

6

Miracle on Crack Alley

For more than five months, I, along with a handful of volunteers, worked day after day doing demo work on the Clinton property. This included removing everything—all the lath and plaster in the walls and ceilings, plumbing, heating, electrical, windows, most floorboards, old roof, gravity stove in the basement, duct work, and stairs. Basically, the building had to be gutted to nothing but a shell. All of this was most fatiguing, but removing the lath and plaster had to be the worst. The structure was almost 100 years old, and back when it was built, there was no sheetrock. Walls were lath lumber coated with thick layers of concrete plaster.

One shovel of plaster weighed more than 10 pounds. Lath boards were about one and a half inches wide and were nailed together every two inches with big nails. It would take half a day to clean out a 10-foot square wall. It was dusty and dirty, and the lath laid on huge piles on the floor full of exposed nails. I must have stepped on dirty nails a dozen times during that summer. I remember the dust being so thick that I could only see a few inches in front of me as I worked. Despite wearing masks each day, I would come home at night and cough for hours with the dust in my lungs. All this dirty work was done in the hot summer months, often with no electricity or plumbing in the building.

Earlier, I mentioned that Clinton Avenue was considered one of the most dangerous streets in South Minneapolis. Notoriously called "crack alley," it was the hang out for prostitutes, drug dealers and gang members. From what I could see, on a daily basis the majority of the people living on that street were involved in some type of illegal behavior. One day, as I was working by myself, I heard five or six gunshots fired that sounded so close they could have been in the room with me. Hours later I heard loud voices screaming near the back alley. When I poked my head out the door, I noticed the whole yard next door was filled with police. A few minutes later, I watched the Hennepin County Coroner carry out a corpse in a body bag. I later learned that a young man had been murdered no less than 30 feet from where I was working.

A few minutes later, I watched the Hennepin County Coroner carry out a corpse in a body bag. I later learned that a young man had been murdered no less than 3o feet from where I was working.

Then another day while I was working, I heard someone calling at the back door. It was a police officer. He told me that earlier that day they had dug up a dead body right next to our property line, and he wanted to know if I knew anything about it.

As I shared in a previous chapter, when I first visited the 3021 Clinton property with the building inspector a year earlier, he let me know that the property had been one of the more notorious drug houses in South Minneapolis. The police had been surveilling the property for years. Fortunately, shortly after I started the demo, the drug activity stopped—or so I thought. I had been rehabbing the property for several weeks now and had accumulated a considerable number of tools to work on the project. Because MNTC really owned nothing, most of the tools that I had at the house were my own. And because it was so cumbersome transporting it all back and forth each day, I started leaving some of the less expensive items at the property overnight. After a few weeks, I felt comfortable enough to leave all the tools. Early one morning when I arrived, I removed the plywood on the window and entered only to find that almost all of my tools had been stolen. Hundreds of dollars of necessary power tools were gone! Over the course of the next three months, items I absolutely had to leave there were stolen multiple times. It was almost as if someone was watching each night when I would leave. It was one discouragement after another.

It was almost as if someone was
watching each night when
I would leave.

It would be 25 years later at one of our all-staff trainings at MNTC that the rest of the story would be told. At this particular training with about 300 staff members in the room and online, the leadership honored Lynette's and my 25 years of service. Staff thanked us, presented a gift, and just before we were to dismiss, our men's program director came to the microphone and asked if he could say one final word. He pointed out to one of our head chaplains—a very dedicated worker—and said, "Pastor Rich, before you leave, Pastor Ronnie wants to make a confession. He didn't have the nerve to say it himself, so he asked me to ask you if you would please forgive him? He wants you to know that 25 years ago, HE was the drug addict living in the abandoned structure right next to the 3021 Clinton Avenue house you were working on. And HE was the one who would watch for you to leave so he could break in and steal all your tools." This brought tears to my eyes—not in anger, but in gratitude.

Ronnie had entered our program 15 years earlier as a homeless and hopeless heroin addict. He came to us right out of jail in a wheelchair, unable to walk because his feet were so frostbitten that the doctors were considering amputation. Miraculously, during the months at MNTC, the feeling came back into his feet, and he was healed. He graduated from our program and stayed on to help us. He later worked on his clergy license, started a church in south Minneapolis and became one of our senior chaplains. Today he continues to be a highly respected member of our staff. I have since said that it would have been worth a thousand break-ins for one trophy like him. But 25 years ago, it was not a laughable experience.

Back during the Clinton renovation, another huge obstacle the city brought to my attention was the flight of stairs leading to the second floor. The length of the stairs exceeded the length currently allowed by the city. Remember, when a building is condemned by the city, it has to be rebuilt to match current code requirements. Nothing is grandfathered in. The city engineers were requiring me to build a platform halfway up the stairs to break up the length. The problem was that we had no room available. I had an architect examine the dilemma, and he told me that the only way to fix this problem was to completely gut all existing walls in the entire four-plex and redesign everything. This would have added tens of thousands of dollars onto the project and greatly reduced the living space in each of the units. It also potentially required relocating all four main bathrooms. After several meetings with the architect, I left feeling hopeless.

One of our larger supporting churches while I was in Africa was, and continues to be, Emmanuel Christian Center. I'd heard that they had a large men's group that often helped with church construction, so I invited their leadership over to look at our Clinton project. Interestingly, when we finally were able to coordinate their site visit weeks later, I had just returned from meeting the Minneapolis Planning Department about the stair length issue. During that tour, I shared my concern with the group. One of the men just happened to own one of the largest architect and construction companies in the Twin Cities. "I have an idea," he said. I was surprised. What could he be thinking? I had met with our architect multiple times about this, and each time I was told that there was nothing we could do except build a platform halfway up the stairs. He offered to schedule a meeting down-town with the planning department and invited me to join him.

When he and the planner saw each other, they talked like old friends. They went into the planner's office and came out 15 min-utes later saying, "It is all fixed. Let's go."

On the way out to the car I was flabbergasted. "How did you do this?"

"The planner and I worked together for years, and I was his boss." He went on to explain that the steps were too long by only a few inches, and by reconfiguring and redesigning the steps it would be an easy fix. I was actually able to fix the problem in just a few days. What the members of the planning department and our architect couldn't figure out (except for gutting the whole build-ing), this volunteer figured out in five minutes. God is so good! Whenever I was up against a wall with no answer in sight, God would always come through with a ray of hope. This may have been just a staircase, but it was a huge miracle for me at that time.

Although the Lord had come through on our stairs issue, I still had no idea how we were going to move forward on the more expensive projects that required licensed contractors. Borrowing the money was not an option. With very little support coming in through donations, I was not going to allow the ministry to dig a deeper hole than what it was already in. Since starting the demo project, it was constant survival from hand to mouth. Each week I would try to schedule a service on Sunday to talk about the proj-ect. The offerings from these services would help fund the work that needed to be done the next week. Some of these offerings barely covered the cost of going out to the church and back.

One Sunday, I was able to schedule a service at a small church about two hours away, near Brainerd, Minnesota. The church was *very* rural—pretty much out in the middle of nowhere. That Sunday, about 25 people showed up for the service. At the conclusion, the pastor joyfully handed me a small offering. He was very excited because he knew that his people had sacrificed to make this happen. At this church, I also met a man who introduced himself as a businessman who owned a lumber business. He said that he cut his own wood and could give me two by four and one by six boards if I could use them. I was thrilled because we needed lumber badly! He also offered to bring a semi full of them down the next week.

On the long drive home that morning, I remember thinking about the service. The trip took up most of the day, and the offering – even though it was sacrificial – barely covered my travel expenses. But if I could get a semi of lumber from the trip, it was truly worth it. I waited with anticipation. Later that week as I was working on the house, I heard a large semi-truck stop right in front of the property. Expectantly, I ran outside to receive our desperately needed donation only to find out that it was a semi loaded with heavy wooden pallets (the kind to haul heavy items). They were made of a number of smaller boards nailed together, and to extract the lumber meant that I would have to spend days tearing each of them apart. Standing out in front of the load was the businessman whom I had met days earlier.

As I looked over the load, I tried not to show my disappointment. We unloaded the pallets into the backyard, and I, along with a few volunteers, started the exhaustive project of trying to dismantle them. Much of the wood on the pallets was so broken up by the time we finally were able to pull them apart, it was hardly worth the effort. On top of this, each board was only four feet long. What can you do with a four-foot board? This whole thing seemed like another major disappointment.

After several months, I received notice from the City of Minneapolis saying that my demo permit was ready to expire. When I went in to talk with them, they wanted me to start making applications for my construction permits. They reminded me that all electrical, plumbing, and heating work had to be done by licensed contractors. I let them know that I had started acquiring multiple quotes, and we were getting close to locking in the contractors. What I didn't let them know was that we didn't have a penny to hire anyone. Things were beginning to look impossible.

I had started acquiring quotes just to get ideas of the costs. The electrical quotes were all coming in over $15,000, plumbing quotes over $15,000, heating quotes of $18,000, roof repair was $20,000, and windows were $20,000. When you add new doors and hardware, flooring, sheetrock, bathroom and kitchen cabinets, carpet and tile, stucco repairs, light fixtures, paint, and appliances, we were now looking at well over $125,000. This isn't a lot of construction money today, but back then it was huge! And it was 125,000 more dollars than we had.

Each of the contractors who came over for bids would hear my appeal for help with the project. One of these contractors was a referral from an employee of a company in the Twin Cities. I had met him at one of the churches I'd visited one Sunday. He explained to me that the owner of this large company gave to a lot of Christian causes and encouraged me to visit him. The employee also said he would offer his services free if the contractor would allow him to help. Later that week, I decided to meet with the contractor. As we met, he let me know that he knew a little of the history of MNTC and said he would like to help. Being emboldened by desperation, I came right out and asked if he could donate the total amount of the supplies and service to help MNTC.

I think he was a little taken aback by my request. He took a breath, smiled, and said, "Unfortunately, I am not in the position to do the whole amount." I then told him that one of his employees had offered to donate his time to help with the project if he allowed it and pulled the permits. To that, the owner let me know that his construction union would probably not allow this, but he would check. He also assured me that his company would be there to help, and that he would send out his project manager in a few days to inspect the work and get back to me. He assured me that he wanted to help and would do his best.

It was several weeks after his project manager had stopped by that I was working in one of the back bedrooms pulling plaster and lath off the ceiling. It was around the end of August, and it had been extremely hot the whole week. All of the windows on the Clinton property were covered with plywood, and because I worked most days alone, I seldom took the plywood off. Trying to put the large sheets of plywood back on by myself at the end of the day was nearly impossible. And because plywood covered the windows, there was absolutely no fresh air flow. When you add the dust from tearing off the lath and plaster and the exhausting heat in the boarded-up room, working conditions were horrible. To make matters worse, that day I had been pulling lath and plaster off the ceiling. Anyone who has ever done this will tell you that it is a dangerous, dirty, and exhausting job. When the plaster falls off of the lath, it often falls down in large chunks. These chunks of concrete plaster are heavy, and if they hit you on the head, they are sharp and cutting.

That day, I remember the room was very dusty. I couldn't see more than two feet in front of my face, and I was balancing on a very tippy ladder that was mounted on top of about three feet of broken lath and plaster. The only light I had was from a small, dented lamp that had been left with the property. I was hot and sweaty, completely covered in dust and dirt, bleeding from my head where I had been hit by falling plaster, and so very tired (emotionally and physically). All of a sudden, someone stepped into the dark room. It was the woman who, for a few days each week, helped with the MNTC office work. She had brought over a stack of mail. As I looked over the contents, I noticed the quote from the Christian contractor that I had been waiting for.

I was so excited! Would this finally be the miracle that I had been praying for? Tearing the envelope open and lifting the contents up to the lamp, I couldn't believe my eyes. Of the six or seven quotes that I had gathered for this project, his quote was the most expensive! It caught me completely off guard. Over the years I have reflected back on this moment hundreds of times.

Would this finally be the miracle that I had been praying for? Tearing the envelope open and lifting the contents up to the lamp, I couldn't believe my eyes.

What happened next would become a milestone in my 50 years of ministry experience. I've never been intimidated by struggles. From 1993 to 1995, I traveled across America doing missions work on Native American reservations and migrating labor camps, accompanied with street ministry. During these years, I never once was paid anything. I remember ministering in Montana on a Native American Reservation where, for days on end, all we had to eat were potatoes. In 1978, I took over the pastorate of a church in northern Minnesota that had recently split right down the middle. And trust me, no one wanted to take that assignment!

We spent years working inside South Africa's segregated townships during the apartheid period, the most violent time in South Africa's history. During the seven years we served as missionaries, our family of four netted $850 a month. This was during a time when America had sanctions on South Africa. We would end up paying double for many things over there compared to what people paid here. So, I understand hardships!

However, in all of our years of ministry, I never remember being this discouraged. As I held onto the quote, tears welled up in my eyes. I'd been praying, hoping, and believing that this would be the first great miracle that we were about to see, but now it is just another huge disappointment–a sucker punch. This quote was almost insulting. It was substantially higher than the others.

Something inside of me snapped that afternoon. Physically, emotionally, and even spiritually I had reached the end. Like a rubber band that can only stretch so far before something breaks, I had just stretched beyond my limit.

Something inside of me snapped that afternoon. Physically, emotionally, and even spiritually I had reached the end.

I remember yelling out to God saying, "Where are you? Don't you care?" I began ripping up the quote in utter disgust, telling God that I was done with His Teen Challenge. With every tear my decision to quit was becoming more and more real! I was dead serious, fed up with the whole thing, and finally—*finally*—walking away. There were so many factors that had been building for months. People I had expected to lend a hand never showed up once to help. Many of my supporting churches had now dropped us since we were no longer on 'foreign soil'. I inherited a ministry with huge debt and a horrible reputation. Some pastors who had dropped their support were saying their leadership was questioning whether Minnesota even needed a Teen Challenge. The lawsuits concerning my predecessor's actions were progressing. The city was putting pressure on me to start moving forward with the construction, heating, electrical, and plumbing permits, and we were still broke.

And the last unbearable straw—I was feeling that even God could not have cared less if this thing succeeded or failed. I was discouraged and heartbroken. My tears turned into open weeping, then into deep, inconsolable sobs. Honestly, for maybe 15 minutes I was bent over in uncontrollable bawling. I cried until the muscles in my stomach began to hurt. I was broken, hopeless, and so angry at the God I had always trusted.

Several minutes passed. Then suddenly startled, I heard a voice at the back door calling to see if anyone was around. From the other end of the building, I yelled back in a broken voice saying that I would be right there. I stumbled my way through the dark, climbing dusty piles of debris from one room to another until I came to the back door. Standing there was an older looking, distinguished gentleman in a clean suit. "I am looking for Mr. Rich Scherber, the Director of the Teen Challenge Organization."

I can't imagine how I must have looked. I had spent most of the day in dust that hung like smoke, my head was bleeding from falling plaster, I had just had a complete emotional breakdown and was crying until my eyes were red with tears clearing a path through the dust on my face, my nose was full of dirty snot, and I had just put in my formal notice to God that I'd quit! I'm sure the visitor was more than surprised when I told him that I was the person he was looking for. I must have looked like something coming out of a horror movie.

He introduced himself as John Koepcke, CEO of Centraire Heating. He told me that earlier, someone named Rich Scherber had contacted their company asking for help for a charity project and looking for a quote. He told me that he didn't usually make these quotes himself, but he was on his way down to the City of Minneapolis anyway to pull a permit on another project, so he decided to stop by and take a look.

As any businessman would, he wanted to know a little about who we were and what we were planning to do with this building. I gave him a bit of recent history of the organization. I told him how I had inherited the leadership with debt, scandal, and no assets. I let him know that we were planning to use the facility to house chronic substance abusers who would be in the program for up to a year, surviving on donations. And then I admitted that the organization owned nothing but an old vacuum cleaner and debt. At this point, he looked at me and said, "Mr. Scherber, how do you plan to pay for this?"

It was a painful question. I had just reached emotional and spiritual bedrock, abandoning hope, and feeling utterly empty. And yet, there must have been a faint flicker of faith somewhere deep down, because tears again welled up in my eyes, and pulling together every ounce of reserve I could muster, I heard myself say, "Mr. Koepcke, I guess we are going to have to believe God."

> . . . and pulling together every ounce of reserve I could muster, I heard myself say, "Mr. Koepcke, I guess we are going to have to believe God."

In that moment, I believe he somehow perceived the depth of my anguish. He asked a few more questions about the funding, and then with a heart of compassion, said something like this, "If you are doing all this to help these people, then the least I can do is donate a new heating system." I wasn't sure I'd heard him correctly. The sting of defeat was still deafening. But as we stood there for a moment in silence, my soul took a giant breath, drawing in the reality that God *did* care. He *was* present. This *was* His project, His leading and His will. And He *would* provide. And what's more, He had just thrown open a window of Heaven and granted our first miracle! A $15,000 heating system! With tears in my eyes, and a roaring fire of faith in my heart, I began thanking him profusely!

Years later, John Koepcke wrote his autobiography, *What's Wrong with Being Average?*. In it he describes one of the highlights of his career:

> *One morning, my business phone rang, and a man named Rich Scherber asked if our company could help with a new project that he was starting in downtown Minneapolis. He said he didn't have much money, but needed some heating work done, and would I come and see what was needed? I showed up later that same day and walked up to this old, run-down house close to Lake Street, that didn't even have a front door. I didn't see any work going on. As I stood in the front door opening with the sun to my back, I yelled, "Is anyone here?" And soon, a sweaty man covered with plaster dust appeared carrying a crowbar and hammer. Rich was working all alone, fixing up this old house for the start of Teen Challenge in the Minneapolis Area. It was a Christian-based company to help people with drug and alcohol problems. After looking the place over and figuring out what was needed, I contacted some other contractors, and we were able to put the heating system in for almost no cost to the project. Little did I know that when I stood in that open door with the sun to my back, to Rich I had looked like an angel, and that he was so down and dejected that day.*

Looking back 30 years, I now see that this event was *the* turning point in the ministry of MNTC. I had just told God that there would not be another disappointment, and He could have His Teen Challenge ministry back. I had made the decision to quit, and I meant it! Now all this happens! Out of nowhere, in a matter of seconds! I often ask myself, what would have happened to MNTC if Mr. Koepcke had not shown up that afternoon. He was God's inspiration to me that day to not give up! I also learned by experience that *when we reach bottom, God is still there.* When our flame of faith seems extinguished, there is a pilot light still flickering with hope. What a God we serve!

Clinton house with new windows and a complete remodel

Burned 15-passenger van

7

Windows of Heaven

As Mr. Koepcke walked back to his vehicle and left that day, a thought came into my head. What if this promise is just another major disappointment waiting to happen? What if you never hear from him again? Sometimes in life things can get so dark and discouraging that all you begin to see is gloom. I pushed those fears aside, and left work that evening with a new ray of hope. I still thank God I didn't yield to that pattern of discouragement! Mr. Koepcke's words inspired enough hope to bring me back to work the next day. And I could not have imagined what God was about to do.

It was only a matter of days later, on a Friday evening as I was packing up my car to leave work, when I heard the phone ring inside the Clinton property. When I picked up the phone, the voice on the end of the line introduced himself as the CEO of a window company located in Minnesota. He told me that someone had called their company asking for help with a rehab charity project and needed windows. This was great news to me because I think I called every window company I knew of in the state asking for help, and no one had responded. I introduced myself and asked him if I could drive out and meet with him in person to talk about the project. He let me know that he was leaving the next day for Europe, and if I wanted to meet, it would have to be very early the next morning.

I was up at 5:00 the next morning to prepare for the day and then drive an hour to his office. I had worked hard all week. I was tired and would probably be putting in a full day with the volunteers that day, and then on Sunday I had a MNTC service to prepare for. One miracle had not erased the weariness, the wariness, or the overwhelming tasks in front of me.

When I pulled into the parking lot, the CEO I'd spoken to was waiting for me by his car. He took me into his office and started the conversation by saying he knew all about Teen Challenge. He had just finished reading the book called *The Cross and the Switchblade* and was thrilled to hear the history of the Teen Challenge organization. As we visited, he began to unburden his soul. I spent over an hour with him, most of the time talking and praying through concerns he was carrying for the business, his family, and just life in general. That morning, I began to realize that God had sent me to minister to him. This was not about windows, but about God's eternal purpose.

The CEO, realizing how much time had passed, looked at me and said, "What do *you* need, and what are you here for anyhow?"

I replied, "I need windows."

He looked at me with tears in his eyes and said, "We want to be a part of this, I think we can give you all the windows you need." I later found out that his company was one of the best windows on the market. This generous donor contributed over $20,000 of custom fit windows for us! God came through again.

Then, just a few days after meeting with him, I received another phone call. On the other end of the line was one of the leaders of a local electrical union located in the Twin Cities. "Congratulations, your charity request has been approved." I didn't know what he was talking about. He went on to tell me that someone had submitted a request to their local electrical union to help donate a complete electrical installation on a charity project for 3021 Clinton Avenue—a $15,000 donation. I couldn't believe my ears. And to this day, I have no idea who submitted the request.

It had only been two weeks earlier that I had totally given up, and now, miracle donations were coming in left and right. I could've never imagined that a $15,000 heating system, $20,000 in windows and a $15,000 electrical system would appear out of nowhere in a matter of days! As you can imagine, this $50,000 in combined donations sparked new life into the project, and even more, *into me.* For more than six months there was nothing but old wooden pallets and discouragement, and suddenly the Windows of Heaven had opened wide!

For more than six months there was nothing but old wooden pallets and discouragement, and suddenly the windows of Heaven had opened wide!

The project would take another six months to finish, but by the time it was completed, we counted over $100,000 in in-kind and cash donations that came in. And as I had prayed, we ended up opening the first home in March of 1993 without borrowing a nickel. God also helped us raise the needed funds and pull the ministry out of debt.

Here's something I thought I should mention – in the after-glow of the Clinton House miracle, we did endure another hiccup. One of our first major purchases after opening the Clinton facility, was a 15-passenger van to transport our men, and I was so thrilled when I was able to find a newer model repairable vehicle with low mileage. A volunteer came alongside us and offered to make all the repairs. Wow, we had a brand-new home, a (good as) new vehicle, and new program. I was as giddy as a schoolboy! We were on the other side now.

That is, until I received an emergency phone call from one of our staff several weeks later. The staff had just transported our 14 men and parked the vehicle, when suddenly, they smelled smoke. Out of nowhere a fire had started in the wiring, and within min-utes, the whole vehicle was engulfed in flames and completely destroyed. Thank God none of our residents were injured. The vehicle, however, was a total loss.

So besides needing another van, I had a nagging worry about the potential litigation looming from the alleged sexual mis-conduct of the former director. If MNTC were included in this lawsuit with no insurance to cover it properly, it could destroy the organization. This threat would hang over our heads for years.

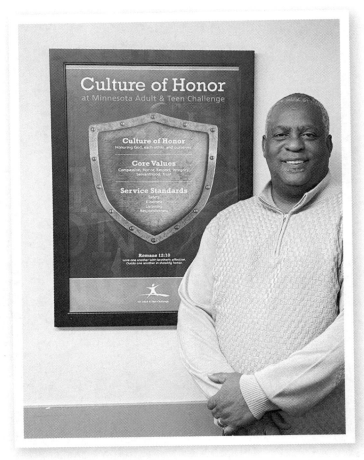

Pastor Terry Francis (MNTC Men's Director) stands next to one of our many Culture of Honor posters located throughout our MNTC campuses

8

New Wine/Old Wineskins

It was an exciting day in March of 1993 when we opened the doors of our new men's home on 3021 Clinton Avenue completely debt free. With donations of mostly used or damaged furniture, the facility looked almost amazing. I found out later that the first home David Wilkerson ever started, nearly 50 years earlier and 1200 miles away in New York City, was also located on a Clinton Avenue! We began with 15 men, and almost immediately the house was full, and we had a waiting list. We had been told by the City Zoning Department that the property was not zoned for a group home, so all classroom instruction would have to be done outside the facility. We found a church just down the street that we could use, and soon we were up and running.

Those early days were tough but joyful. Because we were not receiving any government assistance, and many churches that had dropped support after the moral scandal were reluctant to get back on board, finances were tight, and times were hard. We operated much like a local mission, and much of our food came from donations. Day old pizza from the nearby Pizza Hut was a common noon meal (no complaints, though–the men loved it!). Twice a week for years, I would be at our local Cub Foods at 6:00 in the morning to pick up all their day-old bread and pastries. And again, the men were most grateful for this. In addition, we were able to find several other organizations that were willing to contribute food. Those beginning years at MNTC were both testing and inspiring. We often survived from hand to mouth, and when we needed supplies, we would simply pray them in.

One of the first things we did after the program was up and running was form a men's choir. Traditionally, Teen Challenge programs across the country have performed in churches, which gives exposure to the ministry. Unfortunately, when we gathered our men together and began to look for musical talent, we came up miserably short. Early rehearsals were awkward and often comical, much like what you see in the movie *Sister Act*, but without Whoopi Goldberg. There was no harmony, the pitch was grossly out of tune, no one had ever followed a conductor, and adding insult to injury, everyone seemed to have their own sense of rhythm. Despite this, it was amazing that when the group began to sing and worship, the Holy Spirit's presence would always fall. These street-hardened men would sound like angels! When they shared their testimonies, the miraculous stories of changed lives, and God's redemption deeply moved the congregations. Before long, our Sunday choir schedule was full. Today, the MNTC Choir continues to be an important facet of this ministry.

Early rehearsals were awkward
and often comical, much like what
you see in the movie *Sister Act*, but
without Whoopi Goldberg.

As I had shared in earlier chapters, I knew of the mission,
but very little about the organizational aspect of MNTC when I
first started the program. My previous experience with residential drug rehabilitation up until this point had been secular. Back
in the early 1980's, I had attended the University of Wisconsin
and earned a master's in psychology and counseling. During that
time, I did an internship and volunteered at several licensed group
homes. That training and experience helped lay critical ground-
work, because today we run one of the largest licensed treatment
programs in Minnesota in sync with our long-term Christian
programs.

We have always worked very closely with the Minnesota
Department of Human Services. They are great partners, and we
have always found them helpful and supportive. We have also
found that licensing guidelines and policies have helped steer us
in the right direction and protected us while we faced the challenges of growth. We consider them strong allies! However, 30
years ago, the old school philosophy on how Teen Challenge
residential programs should be run differed greatly from today.
Back then, there were some directors who thought that a military
approach was the best model for rehabilitation. That approach

included behavior modification techniques such as shouting, disrespectful comments, embarrassing disciplines, isolation tactics, verbal fasts, family restrictions, and other methods they considered effective. What I describe next is what I consider to be another major crossroads in the development of this organization.

Because I lacked both background and experience in the operating practices of a residential Teen Challenge program, I felt it was imperative that I enlist help. I thought myself fortunate to find several employees who had previously worked in other Teen Challenge programs to advise me. Regrettably however, their experience was with the old school military boot camp philosophy, one that includes the belief that clients should be broken down first before they can be built up. As you can imagine, when these disciplines were being implemented, I became very uneasy. Having come from a completely different school of thought, it didn't take very long before things came to a head.

I believe as Christians we are to treat others with dignity and respect. I was taught this as a child and have practiced this throughout my pastoral ministry. I remember just cringing at some of the things that were happening, and when I would confront staff members about these *methods*, I was reminded that I didn't know the "Teen Challenge way." The two different philosophies were continually clashing, so one of the staff decided to go above my head and contact the national office. Unfortunately, many at the national office at the time were also from the old school of thought and supported their concerns. They invited a Teen Challenge National Office Delegate to Minneapolis to see for himself. When he arrived, he met with our staff and then asked for a private meeting with the board of directors. Because I wasn't aware of why he was here, I was completely caught off guard.

As he met with the board, I was asked to leave the room. When I was invited back in, he confronted me. There were no accusations of impropriety, theft, immoral behavior, or character issues; instead, it was all related to my philosophy of caring for Teen Challenge clients. I was accused of being soft and not following Teen Challenge protocols! I finally said, "If I am being questioned today on my philosophy of treating our clients with dignity and respect, then yes, I am guilty. This is how I believe Christians should treat others." At the end of my interrogation, the delegate looked at me and said, "Rich, maybe you should consider going back to pastoring or doing something else." To my surprise, at this point the board chairman asked both of us to leave the room. I didn't know what to say. But just minutes later when we both were invited back in, the board chairman addressed the delegate and said something like, "God has used Rich to build this program, and we are all behind him 100 percent. Now you can either leave him alone to be our CEO and director, or we will consider taking this whole organization and disassociating from Teen Challenge."

"If I am being questioned today on my philosophy of treating our clients with dignity and respect, then yes, I am guilty."

I don't think the delegate expected the board to be this supportive or this direct, but in response, he first stuttered a bit and then said, "No, No, No, you completely misunderstood me. I wasn't inferring that Rich should leave. I was saying that maybe since the staff were not supporting him in this, he may consider leaving." I faintly remember a few throats clearing at this comment. The meeting ended, and it became a major turning point for this ministry. It meant the world to me that our board stood their ground on these values. I'm so happy to say that this philosophy still stands paramount for us. The culture of honor stands as one of our most important and endeared beliefs. Looking back now, I know that had the board not stood in defense of me on that day, I'm sure I would have left. I believe the Gospel teaches us that we must treat people with utmost value. "Do unto others as you would have them do unto you." is not just friendly advice. It is Bible. Please read Luke 6:31 (NIV).

The good thing about the whole event is that staff then clearly understood that any type of "old school" behavior would no longer be tolerated. This philosophy was communicated to our clients as well. Honestly, the whole atmosphere of the program began to change. Clients were now happy and excited about these changes, and equally as important, phone calls from complaining family members stopped on a dime. Clients began to realize that we loved them, and when they were hurting, we were hurting along with them. We weren't their judge and jury. We were with them in this. We also noticed that the flood of individuals leaving just weeks after coming into the program also stopped. People now wanted to stay in our program, and we began seeing the majority of our clients graduate.

Since adopting this philosophy, our program has grown tremendously. We currently operate one of the largest treatment programs in Minnesota and one of the largest Teen Challenge programs in the world. I have noticed something else. The programs that have held onto the old school mentality are generally small, seldom contract with county agencies or have significant social service referrals, and the programs that embrace the Golden Rule are the programs that see exponential growth. I think that anyone who comes through our doors for help deserves all the love and support we can give them.

Hudson House with the Stevens Square Nursing Home
in the background

New gym added to Hudson House/Stevens campus

9

Where Soles of Feet Tread

By this time, the Clinton House had been up and running for about a year, and as routine, I would meet with the 15 Clinton House clients and staff each morning for devotions and prayer. One particular morning as we were praying, the Lord kept speaking to me the words, "Hudson House, Hudson House."

To understand why this was important, let's go back in time a year earlier, to the period when I had just begun to work on the Clinton house. A local Baptist pastor heard that I was renovating a house on Clinton Avenue for MNTC and called to tell me that just five blocks away from us was an old nursing care facility that was possibly available. It held more than 50 residents, and the owners were looking for a non-profit that could use the property rent-free. It was called the Hudson House. I got the contact information and set up an appointment to see the facility right away. Remember during this period of time, MNTC had absolutely nothing left but debt and disappointment.

The next day, I met with the leadership of the Hudson House in her office. After introductions, she let me know that she had some very disappointing news. She told me that the organization had received so many requests from non-profits to use the facility, they had just decided to not accept any additional applications. For some reason, God gave me favor that day. After I told her the story of what I was trying to do over at Clinton Avenue, she responded saying, "Give me that application, I guess we can add one more." She told me not to get my hopes up because quite a few good non-profits had applied. I left that day thinking I would probably never hear from her again.

> Here I was taking the tour with these CEOs of large Twin City non-profits while we wouldn't have had the money to pay for a month's electric bill.

However, about a week or two later, I did receive that call from her asking if we were still interested. She said they were inviting all the non-profits that their board had selected to come and tour the facility. They wanted to make sure that Hudson House would properly meet the needs of the organization before they went any further. The tour day arrived, and I met at the Hudson House with a host of other non-profit leaders, all hoping to be chosen. It was intimidating because there were some very prestigious community leaders present. Here I was taking the tour with these CEOs of large Twin City non-profits while we wouldn't have had the money to pay for a month's electric bill.

However, something happened as I was touring the four floors: God began to instill faith in my heart. As I moved from one room to the next, under my breath I was saying, "Every place that the sole of your feet will tread upon, that have I given unto you" (Joshua 1:3). I just began to claim the building for the Glory of God. Hudson House was a small building connected to a larger facility, the Stevens Square Nursing Home. And under my breath I began to ask God to give us the whole nursing home—both buildings. There was such a flame kindled in my spirit I barely saw the mountain in front of me. After the tour, the entire group was told that the board would be narrowing down their decision to three organizations who would then be brought in for further interviews.

As I moved from one room to the next, under my breath I was saying, "Every place that the sole of your feet will tread upon, that have I given unto you" (Joshua 1:3).

I'm not a person who loves fasting; as a matter of fact, it is one of the hardest things for me to do. After that gathering, I felt compelled to commit myself to pray and embark on a three day fast. During those three days, my confidence grew stronger and stronger. It was as if I really knew that God was going to give us the Hudson House building. Day after day I couldn't wait for the phone to ring, and each time it did, I ran to the receiver with anticipation. Sure enough, about a week later the phone rang and on the end of the line was the leadership of the Hudson House. I was thrilled to hear her voice until she said, "Mr. Scherber, I have good news and bad news. The good news is that you were chosen as one of the three main finalists, but the bad news is that we decided not to choose any of your organizations." She went on to tell me that the local Lyndale Neighborhood Association had come to them requesting that their neighborhood offices move into the Hudson House. She apologized profusely and then said goodbye.

I hung up the phone first stunned, then disappointed and somewhat confused. Remember from the previous chapters the continual disappointments we were experiencing while renovating the Clinton House, and now, we were to pile this encounter on top of it! Early on in ministry though, I came across a little saying that I have used over and over in life: "Our disappointments are often God's appointments." This sure would be true with the story of the Hudson House. I also want to say that I thank God for my encouraging wife. She encouraged me during this dark time, saying that God must be working things out here, and that when the time is right, He will give us the building.

And she was right.

One whole year later, the Clinton House was fully up and running with the Hudson House long forgotten. It was during one of our staff morning prayer times when the Lord again started speaking to me the words, "Hudson House." I shared this with our staff and asked if anyone had heard any news of the facility. Someone spoke up and said it had been given to the Lyndale Neighborhood who were now using it for a retreat center. I asked her if she would be willing to go over and check it out. She retorted, "It's a retreat center. If God's speaking to you, then you go over and check it out." We laughed, I shook my head, and we went about our way.

A week later at 7:30 in the morning, as I was driving my normal route to the Clinton House (which just so happens to pass right by the Hudson House), I felt drawn to pull over and park in front of the entrance. Getting out of my car, I noticed a sign posted: *Lyndale Neighborhood Retreat Center.* Seeing that, I did an about-face, got into my car and was ready to pull away, but again I felt the nudge to park my car and go in. I shut the motor off a second time and approached the door, but the sign once more deterred me. Back I went, and was still sitting in my car, when I noticed the Hudson House entrance door swing open and someone began waving. I didn't recognize her and thought she must be trying to get the attention of someone parked behind me. Not so. It was me she was pointing to.

I did an about-face, got into my car
and was ready to pull away, but again
I felt the nudge to park my
car and go in.

As I got out of the car, I heard her call, "You're Mr. Scherber from MNTC, aren't you?" She invited me into her office and began, "You are not going to believe this. Just the other night, my board chair instructed me to get a hold of the three organizations that we had chosen a year ago to see if any of you were still interested in this facility. You see, the neighborhood has not been using all of this building, and most of it just sits empty every day. Are you still interested?" Instantly, I was reminded of my recent time in prayer and what the Lord had laid on my heart a year earlier.

My response was immediate, "Yes we want the building; we need the building."

She then pointed to the three manila envelopes sitting on her desk and said, "I was just ready to drop these in the mail to contact the three organizations we chose last year to see who was still interested." She pulled the MNTC envelope out of the batch, and as she swept the other two off the end of the desk into the wastebasket, she said, "I guess we don't need these now do we? Let's start talking with you." I left her office that morning greatly encouraged and with a sense of expectancy.

While the idea sounded great to the Hudson House leadership, the plan was not as well received by the rest of the nursing home board. The Hudson Building was connected to an actively running 70 patient nursing home for women. Actually, the two buildings were more than connected; they were all one property, even sharing courtyards and green space. The thought of their patients going outdoors for daily fresh air only to share their serene setting with highly tattooed former gang members and drug users did not go over well. When the leadership shared with me the board's concerns, she communicated to me that things were not looking very positive for MNTC. We offered the idea of using the facility only for women clients, and I could tell this softened the request considerably. She told me that she would try and set up a meeting with their board. When I left the meeting that day, I began calling every Christian I knew asking them to pray. I felt certain that God had spoken to me about the Hudson House, and we were not supposed to just walk away in defeat.

When I finally did meet with their board, I brought several clients who were enrolled in our Clinton House Program along with a few female staff who were graduates from other Teen Challenge programs. Anyone who has been around Teen Challenge very long knows that the testimonies of MNTC clients and graduates are powerful. Well, you might guess what happened. Their stories touched hearts. And after our meeting, they asked if I could set up a tour of a Teen Challenge women's program already in operation, just to make sure. Now this is risky business because not all Teen Challenge programs are the same. I really didn't know what to expect! Needless to say, the Lord was faithful, and the nursing home leadership returned with accolades for what they had just observed.

Since the nursing care facility was available immediately, they explained the conditions of use and wanted to know when we could move in. We could use the huge four-story building absolutely free. MNTC, however, would be responsible for all utilities, insurance and maintenance, a cost of over $1000 each month. I was all smiles when they talked about giving us the building to use for free, but somehow, I missed the fact that there would be other financial obligations. There was no way that we could afford $12,000 a year on top of all the added costs of adding 50 more clients to the program. Also, there were issues because the Hudson House did not have a kitchen. All meals for the previous residents of the building were made over at the main nursing home's kitchen that was connected to the building. I asked the nursing home board for a few days grace until I could approve this all with our board and get back with them.

There are times when the Lord puts you right up against the Red Sea and asks you to cross over knowing very well that you will drown without a miracle. This was my Red Sea. Remember, we had only opened the Clinton House months earlier and had a full house with 15 guys. Today it costs about $2500 a month for every adult resident enrolled in our one-year program, but back then I'm sure it was over $1000 a month. On top of this, we had to hire new staff to help run the program. And needless to say, I also had personal expenses; at that time our family was living from hand to mouth. MNTC had absolutely no additional money to start a new program and pay the $12,000 for utilities. As I said, we barely had enough money to keep the Clinton House open.

There are times when the Lord puts you right up against the Red Sea and asks you to cross over knowing very well that you will drown without a miracle.

The miracle I'm about to share is even bigger than I knew at the time because having the Hudson House was critical for the growth of this ministry. Today we not only own the Hudson House, but the whole Stevens Square Nursing Home facility with a gym and full sanctuary. We also own a 20-apartment complex right down the street as well the former Tubman building, a 70,000 square foot residence for women. We did not know it then, but now with 13 centers across the state of Minnesota, this two-block campus has become the epicenter of our entire ministry.

But back 25 years ago, we needed a miracle just to pay the utilities. I left their meeting wondering if I should have been totally candid with them. The fact was, we didn't have $12,000 to spend, and I knew that our MNTC Board would not support adding any debt. My meeting with the nursing home board took place in the middle of the week, and only by divine design, months earlier I had booked a service with Emmanuel Christian Center for the following Sunday evening. Back then, the Sunday night services were relatively small with just a few hundred people. Since our choir was small, just 14 guys, I don't remember if they even sang. At the end of the service, the pastor asked me to give an update on the program. Since members of the congregation had helped volunteer at the Clinton House, I primarily talked about that facility and didn't say anything about the Hudson House. When I was done, the pastor looked at me and said, "Rich, how can we help you? What is your greatest need right now?"

Something in my spirit leaped! God had just opened a door to tell them of the Hudson House opportunity. When I was done, the pastor asked, "How much do you need?' I told him $12,000, and he looked over the congregation and said, "Well, tonight we need 12 people who will give $1000 each, and I will be the first." Within a minute, he had raised the entire $12,000! God had done it again! I shared the miracle with our MNTC Board, and they were all in. Early the next week, I couldn't wait to call the leader of the Hudson House to give her the good news; we would be their new tenants!

When word got out that we were taking over the Hudson House for a women's program, the phone began ringing off the hook. Since there were virtually no local long-term treatment programs available for women, we knew that we needed to get this open as soon as possible. The great thing about the Hudson House is that it came fully furnished with beds, dressers, and other furniture. It was a perfect move-in situation. The only problem we would have with the building was the kitchen, as we would find out later.

Since the Hudson House already had the right board and lodge license for us to use, I thought the City of Minneapolis was also granting us permission to use a small kitchenette in the basement for meal preparations. We acquired the building and immediately opened it up for our first female clients. The small kitchen in the basement was cramped, but we made it work.

Everything was going fine until one day, the City Health Inspector stopped by for an unannounced inspection. He was fine with the building until he went down to the basement. Expecting to see a fully functional commercial kitchen with the usual makeup air unit, exhaust hood, National Sanitary Foundation (NSF) stainless steel appliances and commercial dishwasher, what he encountered was an old electric range, used refrigerator, and small kitchen sink. He could have shut us down immediately, but instead, with a smile on his face, and after taking a huge breath he said, "Reverend Scherber, let me help you." He then began to explain to me that all licensed board and lodge facilities in Hennepin County must have commercial kitchens. He told me that the renovation might seem overwhelming, but he was going to work with us and help me find equipment and installers who would transform our kitchen. This could have been another huge setback, but with the inspector's patience and help, in a matter of weeks, we had redone our kitchen to be in full compliance with NSF standards, and very glad to be so.

Earlier in the chapter, I mentioned that the Hudson House has been a key miracle in all of our growth. If the inspector had not helped us to comply, and instead, simply shut down the program, we could have lost the building and ultimately never acquired our largest residential program in the state. God is good.

The Duluth Teen Challenge with the new
Chatham dormitory building

Grace Manor Women's Home

10

Growing Pains

At this point, the train had left the station. We'd now been up and running for a few years and were seeing the Lord's blessings and provisions on a daily basis. Best of all, the fruit of our labor was evident: hundreds of changed lives. Then at long last, the day arrived when we received news that MNTC was dropped from any litigation connected with the former program director. It's hard to describe what a great relief it was to be set free from this nagging burden which could have potentially cost hundreds of thousands of dollars, drain all the assets we had acquired, and cripple the ministry. For some reason the litigants and attorneys decided to not include MNTC in their final settlement. We believe that it was the mercy of God. Not having this lawsuit hanging over our heads meant that the ministry could finally breathe a sigh of relief.

The Lord added His blessing, and the program continued to grow—so rapidly, in fact—that I began to pray and asked the Lord to give us another building to meet the increasing need. One day, when I was standing outside the Hudson House, I noticed a man working on the lawn of a large 20-apartment complex located right down the street on Nicollet Avenue. I walked over and introduced myself. I asked the man if he happened to know who owned the property. "I'm the owner," he replied. I took a minute to tell him a little about our program, asked him to let us know first if he was ever interested in selling the building, and then left.

It was just a few weeks later that he got in touch with me saying he had thought about it, and he was now planning to sell. I'm sure you know that 20 apartment complex buildings are not cheap. Also, this complex was less than 30 years old. When he told me that he would like to help MNTC and offered to sell it to us for only $300,000, I couldn't believe my ears. I immediately said that I was very interested and asked for a several month grace period, so I could try to acquire the money. The owner was most gracious and agreed to give us the needed time.

Now remember, I don't like the idea of taking out mortgages. I thank God that the board was also of this same persuasion. Truthfully, this project could have easily justified borrowing the money. We needed the space now, the price was incredible, and the Clinton property was all paid off, creating collateral against the $300,000. However, in hindsight if we would have taken out the loan, it most likely would have hindered us from stepping into a future building which would be critical to keep the pace of our rapid growth.

Since our ministry in Africa had always been vastly fruitful, and I had raised all my own support, I am not afraid to ask for help. I have always believed that where God guides, He also provides. After receiving approval from the board to move forward with purchasing this apartment complex, I immediately started setting up donor meetings. God blessed those efforts. In just a few months, the $300,000 was raised, and we proceeded with the purchase.

Unfortunately, though, when we finally came to the closing, half the tenants still had leases and had to be allowed to stay for several months. Thus began another nightmare in the saga of MNTC. Most of these remaining tenants were serious drug users, and those who were around the building on the weekends and evenings witnessed that it was a very dangerous place to be. Every time I drove in front of the building, I could see 20 to 30 gang members hanging out on the lawn. Even our staff members were afraid to go near the place. I tried to hire someone to watch the building, but even the security worker was scared off. For six months, the building became a haven of drug activity. All the apartments were being broken into and trashed, homeless people were being let in every night, no one would pay their rent, and one morning I arrived to find that all the copper had been stripped from the laundry area. I began to understand why the owner couldn't wait to sell and gave us such a great price.

Every time I drove in front of the building, I could see 20 to 30 gang members hanging out on the lawn. Even our staff members were afraid to go near the place.

Those six months seemed like a lifetime, but in the end, the leases expired. And after every last person left, we were able to start renovation. Sadly, the last few tenants were angry about being forced to leave, and really trashed the place—to the point of ripping plumbing off the wall causing flooding. Needless to say, we ended up gutting nearly all of the apartments. Our first undertaking (after resolving the plumbing issues) was to remove the carpets. You wouldn't think something that simple would cause us to hit another roadblock, but in about half of the apartments the workers encountered so much loose cocaine in the rugs that the powder was making them ill, and some were getting dazed by the drugs. For their protection, I let them go. Then I put my face mask back on and worked until the last carpet was cleared out.

After about six months of arduous work, and with the help of dedicated volunteers, the Nicollet building was fresh and ready for occupancy. Let me tell you, it was a happy day for all of us when we temporarily transitioned the men over from the Clinton property. And I say temporarily, because eventually we were able to sell that building at three times our purchase price in order to buy the Hudson House and the entire Stevens Square Nursing Home, our largest campus to date.

In 2006, we watched the Lord open two brand new centers completely unexpectedly. They were the Grace Manor Women's Home and the Duluth Teen Challenge, both within a matter of months.

The first was Grace Manor. Early in the last century, Mrs. Emily Holmquist opened Grace Manor in north Minneapolis because she was burdened by the increasing number of aging individuals in the city needing love, care, and housing. Originally called the Scandinavian Union Relief Home, it went through a number of transitions over the years, but in 2005, Teen Challenge was approached to see if we were interested occupying the entire campus. I'm glad to report that at any given time for the past 16 years, this incredible mansion has been the home for up to 50 women in need of our help. God is good!

Then came the Duluth campus. As far back as I can remember, this community had been asking us to establish a program there. Duluth is a port community on the tip of Lake Superior with a population of 86,697 making it Minnesota's fourth-largest city. Because Lynette grew up near there and we had been pastors in the area for seven years, that neck of the woods has always been dear to our hearts.

During our stay in northern Minnesota, I also volunteered at a local drug treatment facility and saw firsthand the desperate need. Because my heart was already softened, it didn't take much persuasion when members of the community began to contact us asking for help. Saint Louis County has the highest opioid drug overdose rates in the state.

After several unsuccessful starts, the subject of expansion into the Northland resurfaced with a phone call from a Duluth resident who I had never met before. He was very insistent that we reconsider helping the area and wanted to show us a property.

I would have said no except that God had been stirring something in my heart. I just felt like I was supposed to invite a few donors to join us for the tour. The building that was for sale was a former YMCA building off Lake Avenue in downtown Duluth. Even though it was not set up as a board and lodge facility, it had potential. It had a large gym and exercise area, several classrooms,

offices, a large reception area, dormitory space and room for a cafeteria and kitchen. It wasn't perfect, but we could make it work.
I loved the location because it sat high on the hill overlooking
beautiful Lake Superior.

After touring the building, we headed straight back to
Minneapolis. In the car we talked a little about the possibility
with the building, but soon the subject turned elsewhere. Since
both of the people who accompanied me to Duluth had parked at
my office, I asked them if they wanted to come in for a tour. They
agreed, and I took them for a short visit of the program and then
introduced them to a couple residents who quickly shared their
testimonies. It was now time for them to go, but the donor asked
if he could use my office alone for a minute. I wasn't sure what
he wanted, but he asked his friend to join him. The two of them
went into my office and came out about five minutes later with
big smiles on their faces. They said, "We have great news, and you
might want to sit down, because the two of us are each going to go
in for half, and we are going to buy the Duluth building for you." I
couldn't believe my ears! God had done it again!

Since then, the Duluth campus has had several changes, the
greatest being the addition of the Chatham Building, a four-story
21-unit apartment complex connected to our current campus by
a double wall. We eventually purchased it and fully integrated the
two structures. This was another great blessing because the original Duluth building had been a YMCA. There were no private
bedrooms, and residents were required to live together in large
dormitory spaces. With the addition of the apartment building,
we were able to open up the walls between the buildings and add
necessary bedroom and private living areas. Today, the Duluth

campus remains full continually and has been a lighthouse to those whose lives have been shipwrecked as a result of addiction.

1619 Portland Avenue men's facility

June 26, 1998, inside the building

11

Pushing Back the Darkness

I t was sometime back in 1996 that I received a call out of the blue from a real estate agent letting me know that a large building which formerly housed a Bible college was becoming available not far from us. Since his call was just months after we had moved into the 20-apartment complex on Nicollet Avenue, I wasn't very interested. The Nicollet property allowed us to expand the men's program, but the added costs of sustaining each additional resident was all we could handle at the time. But the real estate agent was persistent, and after a few months, I finally agreed to tour the building.

It had originally been the old Lutheran Bible Institute and was now a group home for people with developmental challenges. The owners had gone into bankruptcy, and the building was now part of a foreclosure. The real estate agent also shared with me that he was a Christian and had been praying about this building. He had been feeling prompted that MNTC should get involved. I asked him when the building was available, and he told me that because it was a very complicated bankruptcy, it could be years before the legalities would clear. After leaving the tour that day, I sensed an excitement growing in my spirit. The building, located at 1619 Portland Avenue South, in Minneapolis, is highly visible, sitting right on the corner of Interstates 94 and 35W, and I was excited about the marketing opportunity.

> After leaving the tour that day,
> I sensed an excitement growing
> in my spirit.

When I shared this opportunity with the board, they were eager to take a look, and by the time we toured the Portland property, the group home was in the final months of closing their doors. Nearly all the residents had been moved out, and most things were in boxes ready to be moved. Due to long-term financial difficulty, the building was in terrible shape. Rooms hadn't been painted in years, the smell was egregious, and the board was not very impressed. When they asked the real estate agent what it would take for MNTC to acquire the building, he said the owner wanted more than a million dollars, but that it still might be a good value since he believed the property was worth twice that amount. The board left that day, and I don't think anyone thought this project was going anywhere. MNTC barely had enough money to make payroll, much less to purchase a million-dollar building and then come up with the finances to pull it out of late-stage decay.

In the next weeks during my prayer time, I was continually brought back to thoughts of the 1619 Portland property. Weeks later, while visiting with one of my board members who was a commercial property manager and investor, I shared with him how I couldn't shake thinking about this property. I told him that we needed to keep praying because the more I tried to run away from this, the stronger I felt drawn back to it. He told me that there might be a way we could pick up the property, "Dirt cheap, without it even having to go through the bankruptcy process." But it required risk and a lot of hard work. "There are three major creditors involved in the bankruptcy. They are first, second and third position mortgage holders. Rich, I want you to meet with each of them and tell them the whole MNTC story, then see what the bottom dollar would be for MNTC to buy out their position in the bankruptcy." He also advised me to not commit to anything, but to simply find out what it would take to sell their position.

I set up meetings with the lenders, and after negotiating with them I had commitments to purchase all of the mortgages at about a third of their face value.

Needless to say, while the board was excited to hear this, they reminded me that we had no money available to acquire another property, as we were still trying to catch up with the purchase of the last building. However, the board seeing the value of the property, gave the investment manager and me permission to explore the possibility. The two of us decided to set up a meeting with the bankruptcy judge to see if he would release the bankruptcy if Teen Challenge acquired all three mortgages. That meeting was very positive! After working with the judge and lenders, within months we had acquired notification that the bankruptcy would be lifted if we wanted to move forward. This was great news and an incredible opportunity for us. When we reported this information back to the full board, they enthusiastically gave the green light to proceed and share the opportunity with our supporters. If we could raise the money, we would acquire the building.

In the meantime, the original owner of the property, hearing that we were looking to purchase the mortgages, contacted me, asked if I would keep an eye on the place for him, and gave me the keys. Because the building was left in horrible condition, I asked him if it would be alright if we started cleaning it up a little. My concern was that the building would become infested with rodents and maggots (a very real likelihood). The owner was more than happy to let us care for the property.

Unlike the two previous projects that we had raised money for, my requests for help with the 1619 project went nowhere. We needed to raise over $300,000 to purchase these mortgages, and very few donors who I spoke with were responding. It was a tough period in the economy, and people were tightening their belts. After six months, we had only raised half of the amount, and then it seemed like things just stopped. Even regular donations were just trickling in, and we barely had enough funds to make payroll.

At the summer board meeting, after examining the financial report, one of the board members suggested that we drop the whole idea of 1619 Portland. The financial drought that we were currently going through, and the fact that some of the staff were convinced that MNTC had now become big enough, brought enough pressure on the board that a formal decision was made to stop any future discussion about 1619 Portland expansion. It was further decided that we would contact the donors who had pledged toward the building, the owners of the three mortgages, and the bankruptcy judge to let them know of our decision. I remember leaving the meeting that day disheartened.

I planned to tell the staff and clients of the board's decision on Monday morning during chapel. I knew that some of them would not take it well. Many of them had donated long hours cleaning up the building, and some of the men had held regular prayer meetings inside the building, praying for a miracle. As I was giving them the update that Monday morning in chapel, some of the men began yelling back to me, "No, Pastor Rich, this isn't the will of God." Others were shaking their heads in disbelief. I apologized to the men and told them that it was out of my hands and asked them to go to prayer (we would always start each chapel with a time of prayer).

To be honest, I was probably the most dismayed of anyone present—not mad at the board, God, or really anyone—just upset that we were walking away from an incredible opportunity. I was a little bewildered as to why I felt so certain in my spirit that God was in this venture. I was staring so many obstacles in the face. Donations were down, some key staff had recently resigned, we had lost several clients who decided to just leave, and the morale of the program was waning. And even more pressing, I was personally going through some tough emotional and spiritual warfare. As all of you know, there are times in life when it just seems like everything is a struggle. This was one of those seasons.

As I went to prayer, I began to weep. Then in the background, I could hear others weeping also. Soon the weeping turned to sobbing all over the chapel. Something was happening on a spiritual level that is hard to explain. I felt impressed to grab the microphone and lead in prayer. As I was praying, I could sense the darkness over MNTC so thick that it seemed someone could cut it with a knife. I began praying against that darkness and commanding it to leave. My prayers turned to intense sobbing, and in the background, I could hear men's broken voices commanding over and over, "Get out of here in the name of Jesus." I don't know how to explain this, but it was like we were actually pushing back darkness! After a few minutes of intense warfare, something broke, and when I looked over the auditorium everyone was on their feet praising God! It was marvelous! I had no idea what had just happened, but I felt this sudden release and overwhelming joy and victory in my spirit. Shortly after chapel was over, the clients went to their classes, and I went back to the office to catch up on work.

> Soon the weeping turned to sobbing all over the chapel. Something was happening on a spiritual level that is hard to explain.

About an hour later, I received the most unusual phone call. The person on the end of the line wanted to know if I was the Director of MNTC and if I was the individual who had been with the choir the day before when we had visited his church. I told him that I was, and then he said the oddest thing, "I need to meet with you right away today, this is very important, very important." I quickly looked at my schedule and let him know that the whole day was booked solid. I asked if we could meet later in the week, but he was insistent, said we needed to meet ASAP, even before noon if possible. I gave in and rearranged my schedule.

An hour or so later, he arrived at my office. He asked lots of questions and then wanted to see some of the programs. During our tour of the Hudson and Clinton Houses, I kept hinting for a reason why he wanted to meet, but he wouldn't tell me. Somehow, just from the way he was asking questions, I sensed that just maybe, he was interested in making a contribution. On the way back from the Clinton house, we took a detour and parked right in front of 1619 Portland. I spent the next 15 minutes telling him the whole story of what we had just gone through with what had originally been the Lutheran Bible Institute. I told him about the real estate agent who kept calling me saying he felt God wanted us to get this property. I told him how we had spent three months cleaning up the mess left behind, and how the staff and clients would have prayer meetings inside, and how they would come back saying God had spoken to them that we were supposed to get the building.

I shared with him how I had visited the three creditors in the bankruptcy proceedings, and how they were willing to sell their positions to us, about our very positive meeting with the judge, and finally, how the board, on Friday, had decided to back out of the purchase because we just couldn't raise the balance of the money. When I finished, all he did was smile. With no other response, I started the car up, and we headed back to my office.

Just as I was exiting the car, he asked me to wait. He seemed very touched, nearly to the point of tears. He told me that he had been in the congregation when the choir shared the day before, and that the Holy Spirit had spoken to him to give a sizable gift to the ministry. "But I didn't do it," he confessed, and with that he reached in his pocket and pulled out a check and handed it to me. He began to tell the story, how just an hour or so earlier, before calling me that morning, God had spoken to him! He said, "God wants me to give you this check, and I have to do it now." When I opened the check to see the amount, I couldn't believe it. His donation was almost exactly the amount we needed to finish the purchase of the three mortgages and acquire the building!

When I opened the check to see the amount, I couldn't believe it.

After he left, I had a greater understanding of what had happened earlier that morning in chapel. In the Bible there are many stories of the power of prayer intercession. Those who prevailed in prayer often saw the miracle. That was the miracle offering that helped us to acquire the building which has been the home to 100 men at any given time for more than 15 years. The building is such a blessing because it not only houses so many individuals, but it also has all the needed offices, classrooms, recreation space, and chapel areas. It was, and continues to be, a miracle building!

12

Sharpening Our Axe

I heard a story once about a woodcutter who began cutting wood very quickly, but as he continued, the work became slower and more tedious until, at length, he produced very little and was most discouraged. He approached his employer and was given this advice: sharpen your axe!

As I am writing this book, there are more than 1600 residential Teen Challenge programs worldwide. Since their inception 60 years ago, they have grown to become the world's largest drug addiction recovery program. Through the years, Teen Challenge has also gained a recognized reputation for their success. The acclaim can be attributed to two main reasons: their long-term, 12-month residential model, and then most importantly, their faith-based approach. From the beginning, Christianity has been at the core of the foundation. Many Teen Challenge leaders believe that by developing a personal relationship with Christ, and by following Biblical instruction, one can gain all the tools necessary to overcome addiction.

The founder, David Wilkerson, was a pastor and an evangelist. He had no clinical experience but gained worldwide attention for his success using just this Biblical approach. Across the globe, most Teen Challenge Programs operate like Gospel missions and take limited government funding. Because of the strong connection that Teen Challenge has with Christian ministry and the church, licensed treatment has often been looked upon as taboo, unnecessary, and even—in some circles—a hostile concept.

> ... licensed treatment has often been
> looked upon as taboo, unnecessary,
> and even—in some circles—
> a hostile concept.

I will admit, I held this same 'unnecessary' attitude when I first started the ministry. I had contacted the Minnesota Department of Human Services (DHS) when I first started the MNTC program to make sure licensure was not a requirement. I was told that if we operated the program here in Minnesota like a local Christian mission, similar to the Union Gospel Mission or the Salvation Army, and we took no government funding for treatment, then we would be exempt from DHS licensure. So, this was how we operated the ministry during the first seven years.

Because the name of our organization is Minnesota Teen Challenge, our admissions office was receiving daily calls for adolescent care. I began to inquire with other teen programs across the country as to how they were operating and was surprised to find that every Teen Challenge adolescent program in America was operating as a Christian boarding school. As a result, they were exempt from any state licensure. After acquiring the necessary permissions with the city, the board gave us the approval, and we opened a teen girls' boarding academy using one of the floors of the Hudson House.

The program operated just fine for about a year, until one day, we received a call from the Minnesota Department of Human Services asking about our adolescent academy and our current licensure. I communicated to them that prior to opening the academy, we had contacted their office and were told that there were no licensure requirements for operating a boarding school in Minnesota. They responded that they would check into this and get back to me. A few weeks later, I (personally) received a formal letter from the Department of Human Services informing me that I was in violation of state law by running an unlicensed adolescent program. The formal notice gave me 30 days to make an application or be subject to huge personal fines and possible prosecution. How unnerving! A few days later, I acquired a copy of the Adolescent Chemical Dependency License that DHS was requiring us to have, and then I really panicked. I didn't have the resources, staffing, or talent to operate a program like this at that time, so my first thought was to suggest to the board that we just shut the academy down.

The formal notice gave me 3o days to make an application or be subject to huge personal fines . . .

However, every major decision we have ever made with this ministry I first pray over. I have learned early on in my life as a Christian that when I don't pray, I make big mistakes. As I began to pray for the Lord's direction, I sensed an urgency in my heart not to give up. God began to speak to me about going to see a certain legislator. Now God's timing is always perfect. You see, just months before all of this, I had read a front-page article in the local newspaper that focused on the poor success with state-run adolescent programs. The article focused on a recent auditor's report that was presented at the legislature. The article included feedback from several legislators, part of the Judiciary Committee, who were especially critical of the current programming and were looking for reform.

I sensed the Lord was speaking to me to get the names of those key legislators mentioned in the article and pay them a visit. Prior to this, I don't ever remember visiting the Minnesota State Capitol; however, this would be the first of many times.

I was able to set up meetings with key legislators who served on the Judiciary Committee and were mentioned in the news article. To each of these meetings, I brought with me a few clients from our programs—young adolescent girls who had powerful stories of prior drug use, criminal behavior, and violence. After the girls shared their stories of how their lives had completely changed since coming into the program, I then gave a brief history of the academy. I recounted the fact that I had originally been told that we didn't need a license, and then I shared the formal letter from DHS giving me 30 days to begin application or face prosecution.

When the Judiciary Committee members heard the stories of transformation from these girls, and that the program was completely funded by private dollars, they realized it was a labor of love to help these kids, and most became furious. Their response was, "We have a state-run program with a huge fiscal note and little success asking for more money. And then you have a private Christian academy, with private funding, with huge success, and the state is trying to shut it down! I don't think so." They then called for a meeting with the leadership of DHS to resolve the issue.

Prior to this meeting with DHS that day, all I had ever heard from my peers in the Teen Challenge world were negative stories about their local state licensing bureaus—stories of agencies trying to take Christianity out of their programs and requiring unnecessary policies and procedures not applicable to the Teen Challenge program. So, needless to say, I came to the meeting with a perception that I would be facing an opponent. But what happened that day would forever change my thinking. The spirit of the leadership from DHS towards us was anything but hostile. They were humble, supportive, and apologetic. After some lengthy discussion and negotiating, we were given permission to continue to operate as a boarding school.

Months later, they came over for a tour and expressed their positive impression of the program and the academy. It could not have been more affirming, and everyone left on such a positive note. On the way out, one of the key leaders with DHS asked if he could talk with me privately. He began by apologizing again for the intimidating letter I had received from DHS. I was very touched. He then said, "Mr. Scherber, please do consider licensure. I think the positives will far outweigh the negatives. In Minnesota, we have all sorts of models of rehabilitation. Many are looking for a faith-based model, and not everyone can complete a one-year program." He reminded me that the whole 12-Step Model is based on the power of spirituality, and he felt that licensure would help us become a better program. I was about to find out he was right.

At my next board meeting, I gave an update on the DHS tour and shared about my conversation concerning licensure. The more the board discussed the subject, the more we began to see that the positives did, in fact, outweigh the negatives. We mulled over the idea of possibly opening a short-term inpatient program as an addition to our services while keeping the faith-based long-term program solidly intact. Within months, we had submitted our license application, and we were on our way. Since we were charting new territory and had no one to coach us along, the first few years were a struggle. It was difficult to convince insurance companies and counties to contract with us as a treatment provider, since many previously had known us only as a Christian discipleship program.

Then there were the other Teen Challenge programs across the country. When word got out among our peers that we were now providing licensed treatment, the feedback was generally negative. I began to hear rumors of directors saying we were compromising, following the money, allowing mission drift, and disobeying God. Over the years our staff has tolerated the negative comments about our model believing that we were doing the right thing and honoring God. Again, there were no other licensed Teen Challenge treatment programs to model or national leadership to help us in this area. Our leadership team would learn it on our own through trial and error.

Twenty years have now passed since launching licensed programming, and more than 20,000 individuals have enrolled in that program. This short-term licensed treatment component continues to be one of our most popular programs with an average of about 50 percent of the graduates transferring to our traditional year-long Christian program. In retrospect, licensed programming has helped us gain the reputation of being one of the leaders in our state for substance abuse recovery. I am also happy to report that the success of this model has caught on across the nation. Currently, as many as one fifth of all the Teen Challenge programs across America are pursuing some form of licensed treatment. MNTC has been a model and mentor for most of them.

This expansion has allowed us to give more professional and comprehensive care to our clients and has caused us to grow into one of the largest Teen Challenge programs in the nation and the world, now serving more than 3000 clients each year. I strongly believe that we should continually be 'sharpening our axe', looking for better ways to serve these valuable individuals. That's a lot of changed lives!!

Brainerd men's campus, long-term east entrance

Brainerd men's campus, short-term west entrance

13

Bee Sting in Brainerd

In 2004, when the community of Brainerd began asking for our assistance with their drug and alcohol issues, we were eager to help. To get the ball rolling, a group of local pastors from the Brainerd area began hosting meetings with Crow Wing County and local business leaders to talk about MNTC expansion opportunities in the Central Lakes area.

Now, early on in our history, our board created a list of criteria that would be necessary before we would expand our program anywhere across the state. These were: (1) proof of genuine need, (2) strong community support, (3) an available facility with specific requirements to operate a successful program, and (4) a promise from key leaders in the community for financial support to help purchase the facility and ongoing support for the perpetuity of the program.

As I began meeting with community leaders, it was evident that they were lacking some of the necessary conditions for us to expand into their region. First, they didn't have the right facility, and second, the community had not raised one nickel toward the project. Brainerd is a small community with a little over 13,000 people. Finding the right campus that would facilitate all of our needs for offices, classroom space, full commercial kitchen, exercise space, and have adequate lodging for 50 or more clients was nearly an impossibility. After an extensive search, the only other option we found was to build, and estimates for construction on a new campus were exceeding six to seven million. From the beginning, I communicated my concern that we needed to find a major donor to step up with a substantial gift before we could move forward. The pastors assured me that the community would raise the money, but after meeting with them for more than a year, we still had not seen even one major gift.

Because other communities throughout the state were also contacting me with interest to expand, I let the Brainerd leaders know that we would reconsider starting a program in their area once we found the right facility or had a significant amount of capital raised. Several months later, I received a call from them asking me to come and take a look at a potential building. It was the old Brainerd State Hospital campus which had 10 large buildings, most of which were abandoned dormitories. I was told that we would be able to acquire several of these dormitory buildings for a very nominal cost.

You probably know by now that I wasted no time scheduling the tour. As I walked through the campus, I was thrilled with what I saw; the buildings had great potential for MNTC. The dormitories, although they had been vacant for years, were still in good shape. Most of them were multiple level units; each had the capacity to house 30 to 40 people and needed only minor modifications for our use. The community was desperately wanting a Teen Challenge and promised us they would do everything in their power to make these buildings work.

When the leadership from Crow Wing County heard that we were interested, they also were delighted because treatment services were limited in the area. Our discussions with them led us to believe that we could probably purchase the two dormitory buildings simply for the cost of the appraised land value, estimated at around $30,000 an acre. This meant that for less than $100,000, we would be able to acquire two dormitory buildings and three acres. We were thrilled with this idea! After unanimous approval from our board, we informed the county that we would like to move forward. A number of local churches and businesses began stepping up to help with the project, and it looked like everything was a 'go'. All of the conditions for expansion were now falling into place. It seemed like the Lord had opened a great door, and all we had to do was walk through it.

Since we had never publicly introduced the concept of MNTC opening in the Brainerd area, the pastor of a local church came up with an idea. He suggested that we dedicate a Sunday close to the time when the county would have formally approved the project and then bring the MNTC choir in from Minneapolis to make a public announcement. He would dedicate Sunday morning specifically for that purpose, and then after the service, I could meet with the media to answer questions. Since he had been very instrumental in helping to make all of this happen, I felt this was an excellent approach. We booked a date when we knew all county approvals would be completed, and the pastor offered to contact the local media with a press release.

Months passed, and everything was going as planned. We were now just two weeks away from bringing the choir to Brainerd and making the public announcement when unexpectedly, I received a concerned call from one of Crow Wing County Administrators. She gave me a name and asked me to contact an individual who worked with Land Sales Division for the State of Minnesota. She then informed me that there was a potential problem. I took the information, and in a few days, I was able to schedule a meeting. To my surprise, at the meeting I was informed that the county did not have permission to sell MNTC any of the State Hospital Buildings for the value of the real estate. They further disclosed that if we wanted to purchase two dormitory buildings, the state would have to do a certified appraisal of the total value of the land and buildings, and then MNTC would be able to purchase the property at the appraised value of everything, not just the land value.

When I asked them what they thought the two buildings and three acres would be worth, someone spoke up and said, "Probably over a million dollars." I reminded them that the State of Minnesota had planned to demolish each of those buildings if they couldn't find a buyer, and if they demolished the buildings, all they would end up with is the land value anyway, a value we were willing to pay. Each of their team members apologized but let me know that this was a statute and completely out of their hands to negotiate. I left their offices shaking my head in disbelief! How could all of this happen after so much time and energy had already gone into this?

I left their offices shaking my head in disbelief! How could all of this happen after so much time and energy had already gone into this?

I gathered the board together to inform them of the recent news. We wholeheartedly agreed that we would not move forward with the state's appraisal and recommendation. We did not have a million dollars to spend on two buildings that the state was planning to demolish. And even if we purchased them, then we would have to raise another million for renovations. After our board meeting, I called the partnering pastor in Brainerd to give him the bad news. This was a very difficult call to make because not only was I telling him that the state hospital had fallen through, but also, due to lack of a facility, we would no longer be expanding into his area. The pastor, while being very disappointed, was also most gracious. He understood that it was not our fault and offered to keep the date for the choir to visit his church, since it was just a few weeks away. We decided that it would also be the best time to inform the community that MNTC would not be expanding into the Central Lakes area.

It just so happened that months earlier one of our dear friends, and a strong MNTC supporting family, the Browns, had heard that we were coming to Brainerd with the choir and invited Lynette and me over to their house after the service for lunch. The weather was just beautiful that weekend, and they owned a lakefront home. We were so looking forward to this.

Unfortunately, on Saturday, the day before we were to leave for the service, Lynette was stung by a huge wasp. To the average person, a sting like this is a nuisance. Lynette, however, is highly allergic to fire ants, and the doctor warned her against bee stings, as they are often related. With Lynette not coming along, I was about to go to the phone and cancel lunch with the Browns. However, Lynette—being a trooper—insisted we wait until Sunday morning to see how she was feeling.

The next morning, I had to get up at 5:00 to prepare for the two-hour drive to Brainerd as there were multiple services. As I left the house, Lynette said, "I think I am going to try and make it for the second service." I could tell that she wasn't 100 percent better, but she was insistent that she needed to be there with us. Sure enough, as the second service started, there was Lynette, having driven there by herself. It was a great service with the choir and testimonies, and many hearts were touched. However, the congregation was disappointed when I shared the bad news that we would not be expanding up to Brainerd at this time, but they also understood it was completely out of our hands. Then as we had originally planned, after the service we had lunch with the Browns (Lynette insists I add here what a great cook Jean is). It was now around 2:00, and Lynette became very tired having taken another Benadryl. It was one of those situations she recounts with humor and embarrassment. The entire time the Browns and I visited, catching up on our families and ministry in general, Lynette was leaning to one side on the couch, half sitting up, sleeping soundly.

Somewhere around 4:30, Lynette started waking up, and I mentioned that we needed to start heading back. I got up to get ready to leave when they asked me if I had just a few minutes to talk about MNTC in Brainerd. Now, up to this point, I had not mentioned anything to them about this. So, I sat down and gave them a very quick history of the state hospital debacle. When I was done speaking, Ron looked at me and said, "What about our old Assembly of God Church. Would that building work for you?" I let him know that I knew this building well! It had almost everything you would want for a perfect residential program for 50 guys: a gym, full kitchen, classrooms, sanctuary, recreation space outdoors, etc. The only problem was that we didn't have the three million that they were asking for the building. At that point he looked at me and said, "What if my wife and I buy the building for you?"

I couldn't believe what I had just heard. At that point he told me to go back and talk to our board, and if we wanted the building, it would be ours. When we got up to leave, he thanked us over and over for coming. Going out the door, he told me that he never brought up the subject of MNTC taking the church months earlier because he thought we didn't want it. I often ask myself, what would have happened if Lynette hadn't come, and we had cancelled our lunch meeting? Was her bee sting a trick of the enemy to deter us from meeting with the Browns? Looking back, I am also so thankful that we didn't end up with those old dormitory buildings at the state hospital campus. Almost all of those old dormitory buildings were eventually torn down. The facility we have today is many times more beautiful and functional than anything we could have created there. God is so good.

Over the years, we have remodeled and expanded our Brainerd campus. Everyone who visits comments on how elegant and serene it looks. I think it is one of the nicer Teen Challenge facilities in the nation. This three-million-dollar property has now tripled in value. Out of the 13 campuses across the state, it is our most popular program, continually running at capacity. In addition, the community has fulfilled just what they promised. Every year since opening, their support has helped underwrite the program without any support from Minneapolis. Not having a Teen Challenge program in Brainerd would have been one of the biggest mistakes this ministry could have ever made.

It seems like there is a common denominator in the history of this organization: our disappointments *have* become God's appointments. When a door is shut, and it looks like nothing but disappointment is in your future, we must always remember: "And we know that for those who love God all things work together for good, for those who are called according to his purpose" (Romans 8:28 ESV).

Even a bee sting.

South entrance of Hope Commons
(formerly Mount Sinai Hospital)

East entrance of Hope Commons where MNTC
maintains floors 3-7

14

Perfect Storm

Proverbs 22:1 (NLT) says, "Choose a good reputation over great riches; being held in high esteem is better than silver or gold." As I write this book in 2021, Minnesota Adult and Teen Challenge has grown in size to be above the 99th percentile out of the 31,785 nonprofits in the state. Not only has our organization expanded, but our reputation has flourished as well. The August 2020 edition of *Newsweek Magazine* listed Minnesota Adult and Teen Challenge as one of the most effective treatment programs out of the more than 100 in the state, with three of our locations making the top 10. This was a great honor considering that the standards are high, and Minnesota generally leads the nation in the treatment industry.

This *Newsweek* award was quite a contrast from what the organization looked like 30 years ago. At that time, we were obscure and near bankruptcy. Someone once said that when trust is tarnished, it is very hard to restore to its original luster. However, God has not only restored our glow, but duplicated its radiance to shine across the state and entire region. For the past ten years, we have become one of the largest treatment providers in Minnesota. This type of growth doesn't just happen; it is the result of intentional focus on the things that really matter!

A huge part of our success has been placing our priority on our core values of Compassion, Honor, Respect, Integrity, Servanthood and Trust; an acrostic that spells 'CHRIST'. It is especially important that these values are lived transparently before those whom we are called to serve. This means our clients, staff, donors, business partners, and everyone else who comes into our sphere of influence must see these qualities demonstrated consistently. This means we prioritize treating people with dignity and respect, we tell the truth in love, we honor commitments, and we operate this organization with the highest levels of accountability and integrity. This is the Christ-like way! Over the years, there have been numerous opportunities for our organization to deviate from these values, but we have always made the conscious decision to take the high road. We have abstained from promotional gimmicks, naming rights, questionable sponsorships, merchandise sales schemes, client work programs, or other fundraising opportunities that could distract us from our mission. Early on, we determined that we are only as good as our name, and if that is tarnished, our testimony and reputation will be discredited as well.

Well, these core values would be put to a fiery test in early 2001. A donor who was trying to help our organization brought a businessman named Tom Petters to our facilities for a tour. Tom was touched by what he observed, and when he offered to help, we were thrilled by his offer. After all, he was an up-and-coming business entrepreneur who was well known and appreciated across the state. In fact, various articles and news sources report that the height of his career, Petters Group Worldwide had 3,200 employees and claimed earnings of $2.2 billion in revenue. Three of his largest companies were Polaroid, Sun Country Airlines, and Fingerhut. At the time of his offer to Minnesota Adult and Teen Challenge, we were merely a small, struggling, Christian nonprofit. But shortly after his visit, we began receiving multiple large donations, which we gratefully welcomed.

During the next seven years, Tom Petters regularly visited our campuses. And since he had gained a reputation among nonprofits as a major philanthropist, we felt honored when Tom publicly called us his favorite charity. In time, Tom began bringing some of his business partners with him, and to our delight, they became major donors as well, even going so far as to share with us their business expertise and marketing savvy. As a result, MNTC found themselves highlighted in a number of business forums and popular Twin City publications.

The highlight of Tom's visits would be his attendance at our annual gala. Each year, he would bring a generous donation which he would designate as a matching gift. We were thrilled to see the gala participants respond to his matches, several exceeding $500,000. Soon this event became a million-dollar fundraising night, truly our largest event of the year!

Our relationship with Tom Petters was unique in that not only was he a donor, but he allowed and encouraged MNTC to become an investor in his many companies. It happened like this: early in 2001, another donor made a large contribution to MNTC and wanted his donation to be put into an investment for future savings—a rainy day fund. He recommended that we look at investing with the Petters Group, since many other Christian ministries were also involved, and he wanted to see the best return possible for MNTC. Our board proceeded with caution, talking to other ministries that were involved and hiring an attorney for a formal opinion on investing in a donor's company.

Since the legal opinion didn't reveal any restrictions, and other ministries who had invested were very positive, the board felt free to move forward with the investment. From the beginning, they decided never to use general contributions in this investment, but only the money that was designated by the one donor's rainy-day fund. Over the next seven years, multiple donations came in from that same donor, producing regular healthy returns. It was working so well that several of our staff members took advantage of this seemingly solid investment opportunity.

Our world was soon shaken to the core when the 2008 Global Financial Crisis suddenly hit, creating an avalanche of calamities. First came the drop in the housing market—then like dominoes—the stock market, chaos in the mortgage industry, and unemployment. The financial landscape was devastating! Many U.S. automakers went bankrupt, banks like Lehman Brothers and Bear Stearns would eventually close their doors, and foreclosures in U.S. housing hit an all-time high. It was during the height of this financial crisis that two of the largest Ponzi Schemes in U.S. history would be exposed within months of each other: Bernie Madoff and Tom Petters.

During the summer of 2008, one could hardly pick up the newspaper without reading another headline about some major institution facing hardship. Sadly, it wasn't long before one of those headlines would include Minnesota Teen Challenge. The day was September 24, 2008, when I received a frantic call from one of our board members. He asked me if I had been following the news about Tom Petters. He went on to tell me that a team of federal agents had surrounded and raided his business head-quarters in Eden Prairie, and that the reports were vague, but there were suspicions of possible fraud and embezzlement. Sure enough, leading the news that evening was the story of the raid with reports of possible fraud.

> It was during the height of this financial crisis that two of the largest Ponzi Schemes in U.S. history would be exposed within months of each other: Bernie Madoff and Tom Petters.

Originally, what reporters thought was a multi-million-dol-lar fraud, would in fact end up being a 3.65-billion-dollar scam. It was an event that would become one of Minnesota's most covered news stories in decades! Just days after the story broke, the media decided to highlight MNTC as one of the main charities impacted. I began receiving phone calls both at work and home from news reporters and broadcasters around the country—so many calls that I actually disconnected my home phone for two weeks.

Then, just days after the media began spotlighting MNTC as being a leading victim, the narrative took a diabolical turn. Stories began to include questions about the prudence of a nonprofit like MNTC investing with the scam. Even though there were dozens of nonprofits who had invested, and Tom Petters himself was a favored entrepreneur in the business world where investment companies, planners, and hedge fund managers had all been duped, MNTC was being singled out, and our integrity was being questioned. I would describe this as a black hole in our history. Surely it couldn't get any worse.

There is an old adage that says, "When it rains, it pours." The Book of Job in the Old Testament demonstrates this classic analogy. The first two chapters convey the story of a man who feared God and walked in integrity, and as a result was blessed in every way. However, in a matter of a few days his whole life would fall apart. His neighbors stole most of his livestock and killed his farmhands. He lost his children in multiple freak weather accidents, and eventually he would acquire a painful skin disease and be left for dead. The greatest insult to Job's injuries would be when his own wife and closest friends pointed their accusing fingers at him. It was his own fault that God had abandoned him.

Like Job, the Petters' fraud launched a series of spiritual assaults and tests for us like we'd never witnessed before, and it would shake this ministry to its core.

The greatest test would start with the questioning of our integrity. I began this chapter with the reference to Proverbs 22:1 (NLT) says, "Choose a good reputation over great riches; being held in high esteem is better than silver or gold." Looking back over the past decade, our board has realized that there were many things we could have done differently, but our hearts were pure all the way through. Our goal was always to honor God and help as many people as possible.

Even though from the beginning, our board had decided that no general contributions would be invested with Petters, the media did not include this information in their news stories. As a result, shortly after the release of these articles, we received a number of letters and calls from concerned donors, and finally notice from the Minnesota Attorney General's Office that our nonprofit status was in question. It would take months to prove that general contributions were not part of the investment, verified by an audit done by an outside accounting firm.

Another assault from the Petters incident was the fact that a large percentage of our savings were lost. The impact was devastating! We never could have expected that our investment would be stolen. We understood the risk of maybe losing some interest but never the principal! This completely caught us off guard. Emergency board meetings accompanied by staff layoffs and budget cuts were the norm. At one point we had laid off over 25 employees. To make matters worse, many of our major donors were also investors with Petters, donors who now were in the same boat as we were. In the natural, things looked very bleak.

Now the timing couldn't have been worse, because just weeks after the Petters raid, one of the Minneapolis Fire Inspectors arrived at one of our buildings for an inspection. After completion, he let us know that recently updated requirements mandated every board and lodge facility in Minneapolis to be sprinkled, which meant that fire suppression sprinklers systems had to be installed throughout each of our buildings. Since our 100 bed women's facility had never been sprinkled (it was grandfathered in), the building was not in compliance, and we had a mere matter of months to comply. Quotes for the installation came in at over a quarter of a million dollars at the women's building alone, and our nest egg was gone.

Already feeling like Job, we soon heard word that there may be a forfeiture of one of our buildings, Hope Commons, formerly the old Mount Sinai Hospital. After sitting vacant for more than 10 years, it was purchased by the Fidelis Foundation for the express purpose of helping Hope Academy (an inner-city Christian School) and MNTC. The academy would take the lower two floors, and we would use the top five floors for residential programming and administration. Part of the agreement with the Fidelis Foundation would be that each nonprofit would contribute to the remodeling costs. After we contributed our portion of the costs ($400,000) and construction was completed in 2006, we moved one of our programs into the building. So, by the time the Petters fraud occurred in 2008, we had already moved in 120 clients and the program was going strong. We found out later that because some of the Fidelis Foundation proceeds that were used toward the purchase of the building came from Tom Petters, the building would be returned to the bankruptcy receiver as a form of claw back. When we asked about our $400,000 in equity from our contribution to the remodeling costs, we were told that it was likely that this money would not be reimbursed.

Again, we felt broadsided! Where would we put our 120 clients who needed our help? What about the sixth and seventh floors we planned to use for office space? What about the $400,000 we had raised toward the total remodel? And what about Hope Academy, the largest Christian school in Minneapolis? Would they be out on the streets? This was adding insult to injury! We'd already lost most of our savings and many of our major donors, and now we were losing one of our main buildings. Once more, our backs were up against the wall.

Already at the breaking point, can you believe that only months later we were served by the courts a judgement, or "claw back," to repay all monies–both principal and interest invested with Tom Petters? This amount was in the millions. When we tried to explain to the bankruptcy attorney that we had lost everything, and any funds coming in were spent on programming to help hurting people; our words were futile. Everything had been only on paper anyway, and now we were being asked to remit actual funds. To make matters worse, this multi-million-dollar claw back would hang over our heads for the next five years.

Just as Job's trials seemed to happen one right after another, we too, experienced one major discouragement and disappointment after another in close succession. And like Job, I also had a handful of 'comforters' who showed up at my door, each of them quick to point their finger on the problem. Were we guilty of some hidden sin? Were we just greedy and following the money? Had God lifted His blessing off the ministry? During this season of attack, our whole leadership team did a lot of soul searching.

Looking back now, I think those years after the Petters raid had to be some of our darkest hours, not only in the life of this organization, but for me personally. Actually, there were about a half dozen other aggressive assaults and trials that we went through during this time that I have not included in this chapter. Some of these assaults included hurtful misstatements about our organization and our funding, all of which we were able to disprove. Needless to say, the enemy tried to shake this ministry to its very core.

During these days, our leadership staff established regular prayer meetings. We stood on God's Word and continually sought God's direction for this ministry. I thank God that during this time, we never had to cut back on any of our programming or turn away anyone seeking our help. Like the story of Job, God has a way of redeeming every negative life experience and turn it for good when we faithfully trust Him.

It didn't happen overnight, but as the years passed, we began to see the Lord turn things around. First was the talent pool of qualified board members that the Lord sent to help us. One of these leaders was Bill Bojan, the CEO of Integrated Governance Solutions. Bill previously held the positions as Chief Risk Officer, Chief Ethics Officer, and General Auditor for UnitedHealth Group, a Fortune 25 corporation, serving as a governance expert in both public accounting/consulting and corporate settings. With Bill's help, we were able to implement governance standards that completely restored the reputation of this organization.

Fast forward to now. For the past several years, we have been able to achieve the highest ratings with the Charities Review Council and Charity Navigator which is the world's largest independent nonprofit evaluator. In a recent correspondence to us, they stated, "We are proud to announce Minnesota Adult and Teen Challenge has earned an eighth consecutive four-star rating. This is our highest possible rating and indicates that your organization adheres to sector best practices and executes its mission in a financially efficient way." They went on to say, "Only six of the charities we evaluate have received at least eight consecutive four-star evaluations, indicating that Minnesota Adult and Teen Challenge outperforms most other charities in America." God has so turned our reputation around to the extent that many nonprofits have come to us for guidance on governance. And concerning the investigation from the Attorney General's Office, after evidence from the audit showing that no general contributions were used in the investment, the whole case was closed.

Financially, we also have watched God turn things around. Four of our largest concerns were (1) the confiscation of the Hope Commons building (Former Mount Sinai Hospital), (2) potential claw back of funds that were given by Petters, (3) the loss of our savings reserves and (4) the need to sprinkle one of our dormitory buildings. Shortly after word went out that MNTC and Hope Academy would be losing their home at Hope Commons, God raised up a generous donor who offered to purchase the building back from the Petters receiver and return it to us. An added blessing was that this negotiation on the property took place in 2009 while the real estate market was at an all-time low. The property value of the building then compared to the value now would be a difference of millions. Since 2009, we have expanded and built out the top two floors so that the entire building is now fully utilized and refurbished.

I can say, however, that God was faithful through all the turmoil. MNTC did not lose any of its properties or programming. Pertaining to our reserves, over the years we watched God faithfully raise up a whole new family of donors, and our savings reserves have been replenished. Lastly, a gracious donor stepped forward and helped underwrite the sprinkling of the women's building, so the ladies never lost a day of programming. How could we ever articulate our gratitude? God is so good!

Despite grave circumstances, Job's story has a happy ending. And like his turn of events, MNTC is now healthier than it has ever been. The black hole that could have swallowed us up has been turned into a wellspring of hope and testimonies to the faithfulness of God.

Lakeside Academy

Rich standing with "Cookie Lady" Irene Thiele in her kitchen

15

Wish List

Having a strong adolescent program has always been a passion of our leadership, especially with the name "Minnesota Teen Challenge." In an ideal world, an adolescent boarding school should be out in the country with lots of room for kids to run, explore and enjoy. Unfortunately for MNTC, in the early years, this would not be the case. It was all about survival back then.

Back then, there was virtually nowhere for Christian parents to send wayward youth, other than state run correctional facilities. So, almost immediately after we opened the teen girls' program, the phones began to ring off the hook for adolescent boys. All we had back then were our campuses in Minneapolis, and because we were getting so many requests for help, we had no option but to use one of our existing buildings. We created space by transferring our men out of the top floor of our 1619 Portland building, and we moved the boys in there. While we knew that this was not a long-term solution, we could at least help some boys until we found the right location.

Having teen boys living in the same building with adult men was certainly less than ideal, especially since some of these men had come to us for treatment—right out of jail. While we worked hard to keep the two populations separated, we never felt at ease with this arrangement. We eventually acquired another facility, and we were able to move the boys to a location separate from the adult men. While this new location was safe inside, it was unfortunately located in a neighborhood that was notorious for its drug use, prostitution, and gang involvement. The staff and boys felt unprotected outdoors, and most days it wasn't safe enough for them to go outside and play catch or throw a football. The situation escalated to the point that one whole summer, the Minneapolis Police parked a manned squad car in front of our building just to curb the drug use and violence.

Since the first day we opened back in 1993, I have always taken tremendous pride in the quality of our program. I think Jesus wants—and deserves—the best from us. Our program is a reflection of Him! However, because of our location and facilities, for years our adolescent program was a bit of an embarrassment to the ministry. We watched regularly as parents would come to enroll their son in the program only to have them turn around and leave (with their son) in disappointment. During those 10 years of operating our boy's academy in Minneapolis, my number one prayer was that God would give us a quality piece of property for their program. The need was so very great, but we never seemed to have the finances or facility to make it happen. We needed a miracle.

The board was now spending much of their time on adolescent program issues. Because teen girls tend to run away far more often than boys, our inner-city locations were of grave concern. After a series of runaway incidents with the girls' program, it came to a head one night when a few of them ended up in a very dangerous situation. This last straw propelled the board to shut down the girls' program until we could find a proper campus. The move was drastic, but it had to be done. We all knew that if we didn't also find a proper campus for the boys, the clock was ticking for that program too.

This being a top priority for the board, a committee was formed to work on finding suitable property and to design specific criteria for establishing a teen program. As you could predict, there wasn't any extra money available to spend on a project like this. Even so, when the committee first started meeting, everyone's faith and hopes were high. We all sensed in our spirits that God was going to do something great, and we began to dream big. From the onset, the committee decided to spend dedicated time praying for the Lord's direction on this. Then they met and devised a wish list of more than 50 items we were going to consider requirements for—and believe the Lord for—in this new boy's facility.

As we had no money to spend, the longer the committee continued to meet, the more our hopes for the wish list began to diminish. After a year of coming up empty, we found ourselves looking at anything available. This devolved into a number of worthless trips visiting distressed properties across the state, only to come back time and time again disappointed. At last, one property that did spark a ray of hope was a treatment facility in northern Minnesota. This campus was gorgeous, and the dormitory was located right on a lake. The most exciting thing about it was that the owner was considering donating it to us. After a year of negotiations, multiple visits, and discussions in which our hopes rose and fell, the deal disappointingly fell through.

Still, another property eventually surfaced. It was a former sheriff's boys camp in northern Minnesota, located 125 miles from the Twin Cities. Supposedly, it was worth several million dollars, and we were told that we could pick it up for next to nothing. Upon inspection, however, the property was in horrible shape; the buildings hadn't been cared for in 20 years, it was in the middle of nowhere, and refurbishing costs would be in the millions. Needless to say, this property was added to the list of abandoned hopefuls. Not giving up, we continued to search and found several smaller farm homes near the Twin Cities. But no matter how hard we tried, everything was a huge disappointment. I was starting to lose hope again.

I'd like to take a moment here and reflect on an observation–a pattern I have noticed over the years. Oftentimes before a break-through, one must first go through a series of disappointments. Tenacity, perseverance, and endurance are all Godly attributes found in Scripture. May I suggest that sometimes we settle for less because we don't persevere to get God's best? Experiencing a gauntlet of setbacks seems to have a way of forcing us to flex and strengthen our spiritual muscles, and even more—they serve to provide a dramatic backdrop for the miracle ahead. This would be true as the story of our future boy's facility unfolded.

Now, our committee had tasked one of their members with the responsibility to find potential properties. Every month there seemed to be nothing but dead-end leads. Because things were going nowhere, I recommended the name of a former board member who worked in commercial realty. This individual could be trusted, and we had used him on property deals in the past. The next few months, I waited at each meeting to hear any updates from him, but there was still nothing. With everyone frustrated, I remember leaving the committee that day saying I would just contact him myself.

I phoned the next day and left a lengthy voicemail asking him if he could help us find a property for the boy's program, only spending around $300,000 to $400,000. Several days later, I received a call back. He told me that his firm had done a search, and there was nothing available in our price range that was going to work. However, he had found two former girls' camps, one near Hudson, Wisconsin which was selling for twenty million, and the other near Buffalo, Minnesota with an asking price of four million. Unfortunately, he had received word that morning that the Buffalo camp had just been sold. He commented that it was too bad because it would have been perfect for us. It was 48 acres, located on one of the cleanest lakes in the county, bordered nearly a quarter mile of lakeshore, and retained more than two million dollars of existing buildings. And to frost the cake, it was only one hour west of downtown Minneapolis. When he sensed that I was highly interested, he said, "Let me call for sure and see where things are."

A few minutes later, he called back saying that the camp was being sold to another organization planning to develop the property into a large RV park. He said the sale was moving forward, but since there was not a formal purchase agreement, the camp real estate agent would show us the property, and urged us to come the next day because things were moving very fast with the other group. With that same sense of urgency, I met the camp's real estate agent at the property the following morning.

To understand the magnitude of the miracle that was about to happen, I need to go back to the subject of the "wish list" that our Teen Boy's expansion committee had compiled a year earlier . . .

To understand the magnitude of the miracle that was about to happen, I need to go back to the subject of the "wish list" that our Teen Boy's expansion committee had compiled a year earlier on December 9th. The following is the exact list; nothing has been added or taken away (Remember, our budget is $300k-$400k.)

December 9, 2013
The ideal property for the Teen Boys Program (up to 60 clients, average of 40) would include the following:

> *Located in a rural area (outside of the city)*

> *The property would be located no more than 2 hours from Minneapolis*
>> *Important for oversight & staff involvement*
>> *Easy commute for day trips for donors*

> *On a body of water*

> *Land with woods and open spaces*

> *Existing facilities and structures*

> Guest Housing – for family visits
>> 3-4 small cabins that would sleep 4-6 people for visiting families to stay in (these could also be used for volunteers that visit and stay to help for a few days). These cabins would also have their own bathroom. (Small kitchen is optional)

> Hobby Farm setting
>> Barn w/ corral & tack shed
>>> • 4-5 horses
>>> • Chicken coup (for fresh eggs)
>> Garden
>>> • A vegetable garden, fenced in 20x30 feet
>>> • Storage shed for tools/supplies for garden

> Recreation areas
>> Outdoor
>>> • Baseball diamond (could have a hockey/broomball rink in the winter)
>>> • Equipment shed
>>> • Soccer/football field
>>> • Beach area on the water w/ a lifeguard stand & storage shed for kayaks/canoes/life jackets, etc.)
>>> • Fire pit & campsite area
>>> • High & low ropes course
>>> • Walking trails
>>> • Horse trails
>> Indoor
>>> • Gymnasium (basketball & volleyball court)

- Weight room
- Rec room w/ 2 pool tables, foosball table, ping pong table, tables for cards, couches, TV for video games
- Office space in the gymnasium facility

> *School on site*
  - » 2-3 classrooms 25'x40'
  - » 2 offices for teachers
  - » Teen Manager/Director – house on site
  - » 2 story
  - » 3-4 bedroom (one on the 1st floor for an office)
  - » 2 ½ bath
  - » Fenced in yard
  - » Garage

> *Dormitory*
  - » 15 rooms, each sleeps 4 (2 bunk beds)
  - » 7 + full bathrooms
  - » Office space for staff w/ private bathroom
  - » Lounge area (for TV/video games & couches)

> *Dining Hall/Kitchen*
  - » Industrial kitchen
  - » Dining space for 100/140 people (host weekly visits and small donor dinners)
  - » Office space for food service supervisor

> *Multipurpose room 30'x50' (for chapel, staff meetings, etc.)*
  - » Stage
  - » Sound booth

- » *Large storage closet/small room 10'x8' for storing guitars/drums*
- » *Restrooms nearby*

> *Office space*
- » *Director/Manager office*
- » *Coordinator/Admin office*
- » *Admissions office*
- » *Maintenance office*
- » *Kitchen Supervisor (in kitchen)*
- » *Program Staff offices (one in bunk house, one in gym/ rec building)*
- » *Small conference room – seat up to 15/20*

> *Garage for van storage*

Anyone who has visited our teen boys' property and then looked at this wish list will find themselves shaking their heads in awe and wonder. One would be hard pressed to find a handful of properties across the whole state of Minnesota that would fill these exact expectations. Even if one were to find a property like this, it would cost tens of millions, money that MNTC did not have! Walking across the snow-packed 48 acres looking at million-dollar buildings, I couldn't believe my eyes. Could this possibly be the one? To my amazement, this property had everything that the committee had put together in the "perfect boys adolescent program" list.

Walking across the snow-packed 48 acres looking at million-dollar buildings, I couldn't believe my eyes. Could this possibly be the one?

After finishing the tour, we met in the heated cafeteria to talk. The real estate agent gave me some history on the camp and then told me that the price had been recently reduced to around four million. I then told him a little about our current boys' program and asked him for a big favor. I said, "Could you give me 24 hours before you do anything with this property?" The real estate agent grinned and nodded yes, and I left. I remember jumping in my car, and with tears welling up in my eyes, I cried out, "Lord I claim this property for you! Lord, give us this land."

I left the camp that morning around 11:45 and had just enough time to drive to Eden Prairie for another meeting with a leader of Sea Foam Sales Company. This meeting had been set up weeks before, and the purpose of the meeting was to give an update on a project where he had given a generous donation. As we met for coffee, I gave a full report on the progress of his donation, and then asked if I could share with him a great burden on my heart. He nodded, and I began to share about the struggles we'd had with our boys' program over the past ten years. I then told him about the property that I had just left and how it would likely be sold within the next day or so. I asked, "Would you be free tomorrow morning so I could take you to the property and show it to you?" Immediately one of his associates said to him, "I know your schedule, and you are full most of the day tomorrow." At that point, he excused himself and walked into the restroom. A few minutes later, he came walking out holding his phone. He looked at me and said, "I just cancelled all my appointments for tomorrow morning, let's go see the property; this is more important." Again, tears welled up in my eyes! What was God doing?

The next day, I met the Sea Foam Sales Company rep and the real estate agent out at the property. It was early in December with heavy snowfall and one of the coldest days of the year. The tour took a few hours; then we all met together to talk. We asked for clarity on the asking price and on the sale. The real estate agent restated the asking price and then gave the update on the other interested buyer. The potential purchaser was a national company. Their leadership had recently met to inspect the property and was likely to submit a formal offer as soon as today. With that being said, the Sea Foam rep asked if there would be any chance that he and I could meet with the seller's board and share the ministry of MNTC. The real estate agent responded, "This camp represents organizations located across the Midwest. Their board just happens to be meeting in St. Paul *this week* for their regular board meeting. Let me see if I can set up a meeting with them." He also shared that they would much rather see this camp helping adolescents than used for other purposes.

After the real estate agent left, the Sea Foam rep let me know that he was interested in helping with the property but couldn't pay four million. He asked me to meet with the camp board to find the bottom dollar amount they would accept for the purchase. He also reminded me that time was of the essence. I remember leaving the camp that morning again in tears. In under 30 hours, I had found the perfect "wish list" camp, visited it twice, and now had a potential donor willing to help acquire it. Now, I just needed miracle favor with the camp board.

Later that day, I received a call from their real estate agent and was put on the schedule to meet with the camp board. I decided to bring along several teen boys who were currently enrolled in our program. During the meeting, I gave a history of our adolescent program and showed pictures of the dormitories where the boys stayed right off Franklin Avenue near Peavey Park. When their board heard the stories of the boys' changed lives and saw the inner city conditions the boys were living in, their hearts were moved. I let them know that we desperately needed the camp but would probably not be able to give them the amount they were asking for the property. I asked them to sharpen their pencils and come back with the absolute lowest number that they could let the camp go for. It was all up to God now!

Sure enough shortly after our meeting, I received a call from the real estate agent saying they were willing to sell us the property for 2.3 million dollars, and this included all their inventory on site. I couldn't wait to call the Sea Foam leadership. This was just in the neighborhood of what they were able to do, and within weeks we had a purchase agreement signed and in place. God is so good! I need to say it again. God is SO good!!

Anyone who has ever opened a residential drug rehabilitation center will tell you that acquiring neighborhood and city approvals are generally a much harder job than acquiring a property. We would find that true once we began the process of acquiring a conditional use permit. When the neighbors from around the lake heard that MNTC was planning to open a residential program for an at-risk youth camp, they became infuriated to the point that the local municipality decided to have a community meeting to talk this through with the neighbors. City officials estimated that maybe 75 to 100 people would attend, but the night of the meeting, there were over 200 people there with standing room only. Most of the meeting was to be informational with neighborhood comments. While a few of the neighbor's comments were positive, the majority were not.

Many of the neighbors who spoke that night were elderly, and unfortunately for us, were very moving for the audience. Some wept and shook in fear as they shared their concerns for their own safety, some living adjacent to the camp. Other neighbors who lived on the lake shared their concern that property values would be diminished when this correctional drug treatment program moved in. Others voiced concerns of increased crime, violence, and drug use coming into their peaceful, affluent community. It didn't help matters that many of the properties on the lake were high-end custom-built homes. Many were trying the best they could to be nice as they pleaded with us to just find some other place to go. It was a very difficult meeting because I actually empathized with many of their concerns.

My only response was, "MNTC is not like other programs. We are good neighbors." The meeting lasted almost an hour longer than what was expected, most of it very negative, and I left dismayed. I knew it would take nothing short of a miracle to change these misconceived ideas of our program.

I love the way the Lord works! He always has the winning hand! Unbeknownst to me that night, most of the city councilmembers were dispersed in the audience. They heard every concern, the ones that were justified, and those that were fabricated. Fortunately, this was not their first introduction to the ministry, either. You see, for the past 15 years, every year, a local business called Marksman Metals brings our choir out to sing and share testimonies at their Christmas Party and game feed. They use the local city hall to invite about 400 people, which includes many members of the city council and planning department. Over the years, these council members have heard the stories of our clients and have witnessed their transformation. So, when MNTC came to the city asking for support, most were already on board.

After our turbulent neighborhood meeting that evening, we were asked to meet with the city leaders to address the concerns— both realistic and unrealistic. Then together, working with the city, we came up with a plan of action that would benefit every-one. Again, this was nothing short of a miracle. When the plan was presented to the neighborhood, to my surprise more than 95% were behind us all the way.

There was one other important factor impacting the neigh-borhood's decision. You see, the other potential buyer was an RV timeshare group. Their plan was to redesign the 48 acres and one quarter acre of lakeshore into an RV timeshare lot. Campers and boaters by the hundreds from around the nation would be coming into their neighborhood and to *their* lake. This meant hundreds of strangers at any given time. As bad as MNTC may have sounded, this RV option obviously sounded worse.

We finally secured all the necessary permissions, and the project was on its way. We were able to raise additional capital to build a new dormitory and gym. Church volunteers came in and completely remodeled the cafeteria, administration building, academy building, and cabins. When all was said and done, close to ten million dollars of cash, in-kind, or labor contributions poured in for this project. When it opened in 2015, the new Lakeside Academy was considered to be one of the nicest Teen Challenge Adolescent programs in the nation.

It is my joy to report that there has been a complete attitude change on the part of the neighborhood and lakeshore property owners. Since opening, our boys and staff have worked extra hard to make sure that neighborhood relationships are positive and welcoming. Our boys are especially appreciated every spring and fall as they routinely volunteer to put in and pull-out docks all over the lake. Some of those who were our largest opponents in the past have now become our greatest supporters. God is good! God is so, so good!

Furthermore, I could not end this chapter on the history of our boys' program without highlighting Irene Thiele. Known to us simply as The Cookie Lady, Irene is a petite woman weighing less than 100 pounds who started volunteering with our teen boys' program back in 1996. She noticed that our boys didn't eat a lot of sweets while they were at Teen Challenge, so she offered to make cookies and bring them to the boys when she visited them on Saturdays.

Using her own mother's special recipe, they became an overnight success. The entire boys' (and men's) program was soon buzzing about her delectable 'offerings'. Being a true servant, Irene began producing more than 60 dozen each week. And for the following 18 years, she lovingly baked these in her tiny kitchen and then hand delivered them to the programs every Saturday. Recently, while Lynette and I visited Irene's tiny 2-bedroom home, we toured her kitchen. There was barely room for the three of us to stand. I can't imagine where she would bake, cool and wrap all those cookies!

I did a little math since my visit and figured that 720 cookies a week adds up to 37,440 cookies per year, and a whopping total of 673,920 cookies over the 18-year span. And for Irene, this was just an opportunity to spend nearly every Saturday afternoon with the boys and sometimes men, ministering the hope of the Gospel and the love of Jesus. On top of this, as if this were not enough, Irene was diagnosed with cancer and underwent chemotherapy several times during these 18 years, yet hardly missed a week.

Her ministry to our boys was so outstanding that she won the impressive Eleven Who Care Award, and her story was broadcast on the evening television news across the State of Minnesota.

Honestly, we were blown away when every item on the 'wish list' was granted, but God had one more blessing to add: He stirred Irene's waters and topped it all off with a Cookie Lady…

Our first visit to the (potential) Rochester men's facility

Rochester men's campus

16

A Christmas Miracle

Rochester is Minnesota's second largest metro area. It is an affluent community with more than 122,000 people. It is also the home to IBM and the prestigious Mayo Clinic. It was voted as one of the top 100 best places to live in America in 2019, but it also has a very dark side. Meth, opioids, and alcohol abuse have been on the increase at epidemic levels for years in southeastern Minnesota, and counties are at a loss as to how to handle this. As the positive reputation of our Minneapolis long-term faith-based program began to spread, almost from day one, churches and civic leaders from the Rochester community began requesting our help. And as soon as we started promoting our programs in the Olmsted County and other southeastern Minnesota jails, applications began flooding in. Unfortunately, with limited space in our metro campuses, and because of distance issues, it was clear that Rochester needed their own center.

To back things up a bit, as far back as the early 1990's, I remember meeting with members of the faith community down in Rochester to dialog about possible expansions. It was difficult because even though the need was so great, as usual, resources were limited. To make matters worse, there was resistance from social services in that county to our treatment model. But our vision continued, and over the next 15 years, there were discussions almost annually with donors, churches, and community leaders about expanding into Rochester with a men's program. Like a broken record, we would end each meeting with the same challenge: unless the community meets the conditions for expansion set up by the board, we could do nothing. The two most important of these conditions would be that we find the right campus and that the hosting community raise the necessary capital to acquire it.

As you can imagine, these prerequisites were never received positively. The community badly wanted a center but found it impossible to find the right building or raise any funds. To be honest, year after year of unproductive discussions, I began to lose the vision for southeastern Minnesota. There were other communities across the state asking for our help who were much closer to meeting the board's conditions for expansion.

It was during this same time in 2008 that we experienced one of the greatest trials in the history of Minnesota Adult and Teen Challenge. I covered this incident in detail earlier in the book, but for now you should know that a few years earlier, a new donor named Tom Petters began sending us large contributions. Over the years, we grew to trust him, and another donor even came to us and asked to invest on our behalf with Petters' companies as a way to provide us with a continued return. But when the Petters' fraud–the second largest Ponzi scheme in America's history—hit on September 24, 2008, we found that our savings had been stolen. We thought things couldn't get any worse until, about a year later, when the IRS contacted us requiring that all gifts that Tom Petters had ever contributed to our organization be returned.

Unfortunately, these contributions had been spent years earlier on our clients. How were we supposed to repay these claw backs? Needless to say, the next few years were desperately lean for this organization, compounded by the fact that our enrollment continued to grow. Still, miraculously we managed to survive as we cut our budget to the core and trusted God to see us through. Eventually we were able to settle with the IRS and finally get this burden off our shoulders. To say the least, that was one glad day for us! And even though the claw back amount was substantial, we managed to avoid mortgaging any of our buildings or going into debt. As you can imagine though, it did cut deeply into our reserves, and we again found ourselves stretching every penny as a ministry.

Now, I've noticed something quite interesting during the past 30 years. The greatest miracles have almost always coincided with our times of greatest need. And in each instance, if we would have allowed fear to dominate our decisions, we sure wouldn't be the size of ministry that we are today.

Remember that group of people from Rochester who had been bringing us down for years to talk about possible Rochester expansions? Well, sure enough, it was right in the middle of the Petters ordeal that I received another call from Wendell, one of their search team members, telling me that he had some very good news. I was excited to hear this, thinking that a donor may have stepped forward to help on the project. However, Wendell said that they had found a number of new properties with strong potential and asked me if I would drive down and take a look. I then explained to Wendell that it had only been months since our settlement with the IRS, and unless they had a generous donor, right now was probably not a good time to meet. I knew that our board would not be in favor of expanding right now, regardless of a donation. However, Wendell continued to be very persistent that the search group wanted to meet with Barry, our Development Director, and me to talk about some new opportunities.

It just so happened that our oldest daughter, Holly, who is a physician at the Mayo Hospital in Scottsdale, Arizona, had just flown to Minnesota to attend a meeting at the Rochester Mayo Campus. Since Lynette and I were driving down to meet her, I invited Barry, and we went ahead and met with Wendell simply out of convenience. Although I was expecting to hear 'the good news', he recommended we first take a look at a few new potential properties that were available. Our first visit was to an old aban-doned elementary school located about 15 miles outside the city. It was more than disappointing. The building had been closed for years, producing serious moisture issues throughout the structure. The second property we looked at was an old church in town. I was not very impressed! It did not have the layout or infrastructure to run a residential program, and the building sim-ply would not have worked.

By this time, several hours had passed, and I let Wendell know that I had to leave in order to pick up Holly. I said, "Tell me; what's the good news you've promised?"

With that, Wendell spoke up and said, "We have found the perfect center for Rochester. We have all been praying about it, and we really think this is it." He then went on to tell me that he saved this showing for the very last because they were so excited about it. I responded with two questions. How much are they asking for the property, and do we have a donor who wants to help?

He responded to the first question quickly saying, "They only want about four million for the whole property." The second question was answered as I had expected. He then told me that they didn't have any money available to help. The Minneapolis campus would have to help raise the funds. An answer that I did not want to hear. I think I ended up rolling my eyes and telling him that I really needed to leave to go pick up our daughter. Still not willing to be put off, Wendell asked, "Where do you have to pick her up?" I told him that it was at a Mayo building, not far from the big Catholic Convent, Assisi Heights.

At that point Wendell lit up like a Christmas tree and said, "That's where the building is that we want to show you. You will be driving right by it. You can follow me, and I will point it out to you."

At that point Wendell lit up like a Christmas tree and said, "That's where the building is that we want to show you."

Wendell led the way up the long winding driveways and slowed down right in front of the Assisi Heights Convent. He pulled into a vacant lot across the street and motioned for Barry, Lynette, and me to follow him. Leading us past a large wire fence and then down to a chained driveway, we saw a sign with the words, "No trespassing." Wendell hopped over the chained gate and said, "Come on and follow me." The three of us reluctantly jumped over the chain fence and followed Wendell an eighth of a mile up a winding road to the building. I must admit, it was beautiful! Right next to the driveway stood the famous Assisi Heights Convent, one of the most famous landmarks of southern Minnesota. Originally purchased in 1949 with 138 acres, this wooded area is one of the most beautiful and serene properties in the state. It is also the highest spot in the county and overlooks all of Rochester. People travel from around the world to visit this nostalgic, ultra-manicured setting. I was in awe!

Reaching the top of the hill, I couldn't help but pause to take in the million-dollar view. There was the city with the beautiful convent building in the background and deer grazing in the valley. Directly behind us was the 100 bed Bethany Samaritan Nursing Home that was for sale. Even that was overwhelming. Is it possible God could be doing something this big to give us a property like this? Standing in front of the building, Wendell began to share a short history. The nursing home was only 25 years old, still in excellent shape, and situated on 11 acres. It had recently ceased operating and was just listed on the market. He also commented that it was a very hot property and probably wouldn't be on the market long. Wendell said that he and the team had been praying about this property and really felt that this was the one God had for us. I didn't know what to say except, "Wendell, this would require a miracle. We don't have this kind of money." I knew that whoever got this property for even four million would be getting an incredible deal.

As I said earlier, this was not a good time for us to be looking at any properties, let alone something in the four-million-dollar range. I began hiking down the hill, but hadn't gone more than 50 feet when I heard Wendell yell, "Can we pray together over this?" Reluctantly, I trudged back and joined the group in prayer. I don't remember what Wendell prayed that day, but something supernatural happened. I don't think I even had my eyes closed. I was just waiting for him to finish so we could be on our way, when out of nowhere, I felt the Holy Spirit's presence so thick you could cut it with a knife. The waters began to stir, and I knew God was present. I didn't ask, but I think others felt His Presence just as I had. When Wendell finished praying, I thanked him and quickly left to go pick up Holly. I knew we were late.

> Reluctantly, I trudged back and joined the group in prayer. I don't remember what Wendell prayed that day, but something supernatural happened.

On the ride back to Minneapolis, Lynette and I talked with Holly about our experience at Assisi Heights. And even though she wasn't with us on the tour, she seemed more intrigued than anyone. The first words out her mouth were, "Dad we have to have a program down in Rochester—maybe this is it!" Holly is no stranger to the ministry of Teen Challenge. Going as far back as the first Clinton House, on the days I would have worked all by myself, both of our daughters, Holly and Robyn, would always be there to help. They were there through the whole construction process from demolition to completion. As a matter of fact, much of Holly's adolescent and teen years involved volunteer work for the ministry, including summers and many weekends. She was even involved in some of the expansion meetings that we have had over the years with members of the Rochester community. She knew the history alright! Also, being a Mayo Hospital physician, and knowing the need in that area for our model of treatment, only further fueled her passion.

Interestingly enough, just months before, Holly called me one day to tell me of a conversation she'd had with a doctor in Arizona the previous evening. The physician had recently transferred from the Rochester Mayo to the Scottsdale campus, and just 'happened' to tell Holly about the Assisi Heights Convent and his friend, Sister Generose. At that time, this 90-year-old nun was the iconic chief administrator of St. Mary's hospital and Mayo Clinic. She was a celebrity in the community and carried a special compassion for addicts. He mentioned to Holly that she often stays up late at night praying for drug abusers in Rochester. Remembering that earlier conversation, Holly asked, "Dad why don't you call up Sister Generose and introduce yourself. Maybe she can help you get a program started down there." I told Holly that we didn't have any money available right now, but maybe down the road things would change. Little did I know how prophetic that comment would be! In a matter of a few short months, we would experience by far one of the greatest miracles that this ministry would ever see.

In the Book of John, chapter 5, there is an intriguing story about a crippled man who sat daily at the Pool of Bethesda. Every year God would perform one miracle. Unannounced, He would send an angel down from heaven to stir the water. The first person who entered the moving water would be the fortunate person to be healed. It didn't matter how desperate and sickly the person was; it all depended on getting into those waters once God started to move them. Spiritually, I have seen God do many great miracles over the years. So many of these miracles have started with God's people sensing a moving of the waters, spiritually. The natural mind would say, "If I jump into those waters being a cripple, I will drown." But others said, "God is moving, and this is an opportunity to see a miracle." In the prior four years, MNTC had experienced the greatest financial assault that we had ever seen.

We had no money available to be looking at a multi-million-dollar building purchase, plus renovations. Even if we could buy it, we didn't have the money to open a new 90 bed men's program in a brand-new community. However, if God is truly stirring the waters, and we don't jump in, we miss the miracle. This is one reason why God has caused this ministry to be one of the largest and fastest growing Teen Challenges in the nation. Our board and leadership have always had the faith to follow God's leading even in the most trying and difficult times. We've learned to jump.

... we didn't have the money to open
a new 90 bed men's program in a
brand-new community. However, if
God is truly stirring the waters, and
we don't jump in, we miss
the miracle.

As soon as I was back in the office, Barry and I met to talk about the Rochester nursing home property. Barry is a real visionary and a man of prayer as well. Both of us sensed God's hand on this property in a special way, and we also knew that a property like this would not sit on the market for very long. We needed to meet with our board leadership as soon as possible. I called together our board chairman and members of our executive committee so Barry and I could share our experience at the Bethany Samaritan Nursing Home with them. Cambridge dictionary defines prudence as "behavior that is careful and avoids risks." This is a value of governance that our board has always highly esteemed, even more so after the Petters incident. Many organizations have seen their downfall because they were not careful and undertook unnecessary risks. Both Barry and I knew that persuading the board to look at Rochester right then, in light of our current financial state, would not be easy. The ministry did not have any extra funds available to be looking at a Rochester expansion, or anywhere else for that matter.

As Barry and I began sharing the vision for Rochester with these board members, their first reaction was hesitation and caution. However, the more we shared, the more interested they became. My challenge to them was this, "Come and see for yourselves! Go visit and pray over the property and see if you experience what Barry and I experienced." Our board chairman and several other board members decided to take up the challenge. Sure enough, when they stepped foot on the property, the waters began to stir. God touched their hearts just like he had touched ours. They came back with a renewed excitement in their hearts to see what God could do.

Prudence works on all levels. This pertains not only to oversight of worldly decisions but also spiritual ones, and I thank God that our board understands both. They have witnessed God's supernatural hand of supply in the past and are persuaded that we serve a God of miracles. They understood that just as there were risks with moving forward on this property in the financial state we were in, the consequences and risks were even greater if we were to miss the plan of God. As you may have noticed in almost every chapter of this book, whenever MNTC has sensed God was in a project and we moved forward, miracles followed.

We contacted a faithful Christian real estate agent in the Rochester area and decided that one of our first plans of action would be to schedule a meeting with the board of directors of the nursing home. Because they too are a Christian institution, we knew that it would be in our interests if they understood the mission of MNTC. During our meeting, we were made aware of the fact that they also had financial need. As a non-profit like MNTC, their budgets were tight as well, and they needed the assets from the sale of the nursing home to sustain their growth elsewhere. This meant that any chances of a donation or huge discounted purchase price were slim. They did encourage us to submit an offer, however, and they would consider what they could do.

When we returned to Minneapolis, our board chairman called the whole board together to talk about next steps. After lengthy discussion, they decided to submit an offer for a much lower amount than the full asking price. We determined that if the Lord was in this, He would touch their hearts, and this would be the confirmation that this was the Will of God. We quickly called our real estate agent in Rochester, Al Watts, submitted the paperwork, and waited for God to do His work. I don't think I have ever prayed so hard in all my life. There was such a level of urgency in my spirit, and to say the least, Barry and I were on pins and needles as Al submitted the offer.

It was about a week later that Barry and I began to pray and strategize on how we would potentially raise the money. We both determined that we would do everything in our power, but the clock was not in our favor. Our purchase agreement had been submitted at the end of November. The majority of major donors do their philanthropy at year end, and if we wanted a major gift towards this purchase, we had to start talking to people right away. The problem was that we didn't have a signed purchase agreement yet. We decided that because things were still up in the air, we would only talk to a few donors, letting them know that everything was pending.

There was one meeting in particular that I asked many of our staff to pray about. I was sensing in my spirit that God was going to do something special when we met with this major donor. Unfortunately, the weekend before my Monday meeting with him, we had a huge snowstorm that lasted for two and a half days. I decided to leave the house early that morning at 9:00 to give myself more than enough time for my 11:00 meeting on the other end of town. On a normal day, it should have taken only 45 minutes. It wasn't until I got on the road and began to drive that I realized my dilemma. Traffic was at a virtual standstill everywhere. I had to travel close to 40 miles, and most of the trip you could've walked faster than vehicles were moving. Picture it: by 10:30, I'm barely halfway there, and traffic is still crawling! I called the donor to ask if there was any way that I could reschedule, but he replied that he was booked solid. He told me that he had a noon meeting elsewhere, and if I didn't make it, we could try for another time after the first of the year. Still feeling a sense of urgency, I didn't cancel. Finally, at 11:50 I came pulling up into his parking lot, frustrated, sweating, and kicking myself for not having left earlier. I parked the car and literally ran to the front door and into his office. Thank God Barry had already arrived and had briefly described the project. The businessman was gracious with my tardiness and gave me a few minutes to share my heart before politely excusing himself for his other meeting. We left his office that day without any commitment from him one way or another.

Getting back into my car, I felt like I had utterly failed MNTC and the Lord. Couldn't I have checked the weather report earlier that day? Why didn't I leave my house at 8:15 instead of 9:00? When I got home later that day, Lynette asked how the meeting went, and I told her, "I really screwed it up." I told her about being late, frustrated, and hardly having enough time to adequately describe the project. She consoled me, and together we lifted the project to the Lord in prayer. For the next three weeks, we heard nothing from the prospective donor.

It was now the week between Christmas and New Year's Day, and Lynette and I were down in Phoenix visiting with both our daughters over the holidays. We decided to visit an outdoor shopping mall, and if you've ever been in Phoenix over Christmastime, you've probably noticed that during the afternoon the temperature is nice and warm, but by 5:00, when the sun goes down, it gets very cold—near freezing. It was around that cold 5:00 hour when my phone rang. Outdoors I had a clear signal, but as soon as I stepped into a store front, I would lose it. It was the businessman I had visited with during the snowstorm. He told me that he had his whole family present and on the speakerphone. He asked me to explain in detail the project in Rochester and what we were trying to do.

The conversation lasted for probably 45 minutes to an hour. Every passerby dressed in warm winter jackets stared at me as I shivered in my t-shirt. Each time I would run inside a store to try and warm up for a couple seconds, I would lose the signal. Also, it was so loud near the crowds, I finally had to go far from everyone just to be able to talk. The first 15 minutes were tolerable, but then I got so cold, it was difficult to speak. I was trying to explain our multi-million-dollar project to a whole family who could make the critical decision to donate, and I couldn't even talk. When the phone call was over, I again wanted to cry.

There couldn't have been a worse place or time to receive this call. Lynette and the girls found me and asked, "Is everything all right?" I was so cold that I shook as I tried to share the conversation. Again, I was teary eyed as I shared my disgust with how I felt I had done. Looking back now, I realize that God wanted me to know that this was not about anything I could do; it was all about Him.

It was only a week later as we opened the mail at work that we were blown away by the magnitude of what the Lord had done. Enclosed with our year-end donations, bills, and all of our clients' mail was one particular envelope. When we opened it, there was a donation for 2.5 million dollars earmarked for the new Rochester building! All I could do was weep. God had done it again! Now the only need left was for the nursing home to accept our offer and this dream would be a reality. I couldn't wait to share the incredible news about our miracle offering with our board and all of our prayer partners at MNTC. I asked everyone to pray especially that our offer on the nursing home would go through. I had such excitement in my spirit about what God was going to do next. It was like walking through the Red Sea, with a huge wall of water on both sides and my feet on dry ground.

Of course, we were expecting an answer from the seller the first or second day after our real estate agent had submitted our offer. Everyone at MNTC was on the edge of their seats waiting to hear back from them. Third day, no answer; fourth day, no answer; a week went by, no answer; a month went by, no answer. Six weeks later we were still waiting. During that time, I felt so sorry for our real estate agent; he must have received more than 30 to 40 calls from us. Every time we talked with him, he would give us the same answer—no news yet. As the days turned into weeks, all of our hopes were beginning to dissipate; it was not looking good for us.

Somewhere into the sixth week, I received the most frantic phone call from one of our supporters in Rochester who knew we had submitted an offer on the building. He asked me to quickly go look up the *Rochester Post Bulletin* online article about the Bethany

Samaritan Nursing Home from January 9th, 2013. I hung up the phone and hurried to my computer. There on the front page were the words, "Senjem campaigns for Vets Home in Rochester." As I read through the article, I was dismayed to find out that Senator Senjem (a Rochester area State Senator) was working with U.S. Senator Klobuchar and the Veterans Administration in Washington DC to purchase the nursing home that we had submitted our offer for.

This was my worst fear—the owners were looking to sell the building to someone else. I called our real estate agent, and he confirmed this. He did not know much more than what the newspapers were reporting, but he did communicate to me that things were not looking good for MNTC. He offered to help us find another building if things did fall through, however. While I appreciated his support, his words pierced my soul. I didn't want another building. We had been looking for the perfect property for years, and the Bethany Samaritan Nursing Home was it! Where could we ever find another property with 11 acres, 52,000 square feet, overlooking the whole city, located right next to the Assisi Heights Convent, a 25-year-old building completely set up with a full commercial kitchen, cafeteria, chapel, lounges, classrooms, and bedrooms for 100 clients? God had even brought in miracle funding, and now we were losing the property to another buyer! It just couldn't be happening!

Unfortunately, the next several days were a series of front-page articles in the *Post Bulletin* about further negotiations on the property with the Veterans Administration. All of us at MNTC were feeling a lump in our throats. We knew that the Rochester community would be very sympathetic to helping our veterans, as we were. Also, the Veterans Administration had been looking for years to expand programming in southeast Minnesota, and this facility was perfect to meet their needs. It was a real quandary for us because the last thing we would ever have wanted to do was compete with the needs of veterans. We love our veterans and support them 100 percent. I guess it was a bitter pill to swallow, but our leadership finally came to the conclusion that if they needed the building, then we would have to look elsewhere.

Now it just so happened that two months earlier, Lynette and I had scheduled to meet with our daughter Holly in Orlando, Florida. Holly was serving on the National Teen Challenge Board, and their meeting was in mid-January. We had planned to meet with her over the weekend and visit a local attraction called the Holy Land Experience. Anyone who has ever visited this place knows that it can be a wonderful spiritual boost. God just seems to show up everywhere. That sure was the case the day that we visited. We spent about half of the day going to Biblical exhibits and watching the shows. While we were walking through the park, out of nowhere, Holly said, "Dad, what's happening down in Rochester?" I told her that it was now the seventh week since we had given them our offer to purchase the property, and we still hadn't heard anything. I also told her about the *Post Bulletin* articles.

"Holly, I think we have lost the property." The look on her face when I said this told the whole story: surprise, disappointment, and then determination.

She said, "Dad, this isn't the Will of God! Look how God gave you a miracle donation to purchase the building. You said God was going to give you the property when you first visited there

and prayed with Wendell." I didn't know how to answer her as I
shrugged my shoulders and shook my head. She then said, "We
need to pray." I responded by telling her we had been praying, all
of MNTC is praying. She then said, "No, we need to pray about
this right now." I looked around and we were surrounded by people everywhere. Were we going to have a prayer meeting right in
front of 500 strangers?

"You mean now?"

And she said, "Yes right now." Obviously, she was sensing a
level of urgency! She grabbed our hands and passionately began
pouring out her heart to God. I don't remember the content of
her prayer, but I do remember that it was desperate and passion-
ate. She hardly got the 'Amen' out of her mouth when she said,
"Now call your real estate agent."

I said, "Oh Holly, I don't want to bother him again. He has
told us that if he hears anything he will call us right away."

With that Holly responded, "Dad, you need to call the real
estate agent."

I looked over to Lynette, and with a soft voice she said, "Rich,
call the real estate agent." I picked up my phone and reluctantly
dialed him.

As expected, he told me that he hadn't heard a thing and was
about to hang up when he said, "Rich, the other line is ringing,
I need to call you right back, it's them." I got off the phone and
was almost in shock. Seven weeks and no word from anyone, and
then suddenly this time when we pray—the same minute—the
phone begins to ring.

As soon as I shared the phone message with Lynette and
Holly, I said, "Now we really need to pray." This time I could not

have cared less if the whole theme park was watching us pray; we needed a miracle. Just a few minutes later Al called with the miracle news, Bethany Samaritan had accepted our offer! They were selling the campus to us! I can't even begin to share the overwhelming joy I felt. Now, our third group prayer meeting (in front of hundreds of tourists) would not be petitions for a miracle, but this time tears of thanksgiving! We serve an awesome God! I don't know the details of why things fell through with the Veterans Administration, but they found an even better location in the end. Ultimately, I believe it was God that gave both of us our buildings.

Going forward, we were able to raise all the finances necessary for restoration and repairs, and when all was said and done, we were able to open the new facility, completely remodeled, debt free. God then gave us an incredible director, Tom Truszinski to run the program. Remember how I had previously mentioned that there was considerable resistance from some working in social services with MNTC involvement in the county? Well, I am happy to report that as of this writing, the whole attitude has changed. The support that we receive from social services and the community has been incredible. Today, Minnesota Adult and Teen Challenge is considered a leader in the treatment industry in southern Minnesota.

South view of the Rochester women's home

North view of the Rochester women's home overlooking
Assisi Heights Convent

17

The Letter

Our 90-bed men's program in Rochester had only been open a few months when the community began petitioning us for help with the women suffering from addiction in southern Minnesota. Since we had just completed a capital campaign for renovating the men's campus, I knew that starting a new multimillion dollar fundraiser for a women's home was out of the question. We looked to see if there were any major donors from the Rochester area to help us, and again we came up short. Rochester would just have to wait until God provided another miracle. Never in a million years did I expect there would be a second Christmas miracle right around the corner.

It was sometime in March of 2015 (a year after we had opened the Rochester men's program) that I had a very interesting conversation with a young lady in our program. I was walking down the hallway one day when all of a sudden, a petite woman in her early twenties stopped me. She got right up to my face and said, "I'm Courtney. Are you the head guy of this program?" I wasn't sure what she meant, but I told her that if she was looking for the executive director, that was me.

When I asked if I could help her, huge tears welled up in her eyes, "Why don't we have a Teen Challenge program for women down in Rochester?" She was from Rochester and had come to this program hooked on heroin, with years of addiction behind her. Just before coming into our program, her boyfriend shot up heroin while driving in a car, blacked out and killed himself. This was her wake-up call to come to MNTC for help. The problem was that she had an open child protection case against her, and the authorities were requiring her to go to treatment somewhere in Olmsted County if she wanted to keep her daughter. They told her that if she came to Minneapolis to attend our program, she would lose her parental rights. She had been through multiple secular short-term programs and had come to the realization that a long-term, faith-based program was the only thing that could keep her sober. Painfully, she made the decision to give up her daughter. Staring at me with tears running down her cheeks, she demanded a second time, "Why can't we have a women's program down in Rochester?"

I didn't know what to say except, "Let's pray about it and see what the Lord will do." This wasn't a cop-out answer. I really did begin to pray about this.

Have you ever been so moved by someone's words that they just won't leave you? At that time, we had about 500 clients enrolled in the program, and yet one young girl's plea for help haunted me. I finally figured out why I was so bothered. Courtney's situation triggered a memory of *another* woman from Rochester who had entered our program about 10 years earlier.

Have you ever been so moved by someone's words that they just won't leave you?

The following is an excerpt of a letter that came with that woman's application. Because of confidentiality, I have removed her name and a few identifying details; otherwise, it is unchanged. After reading the letter and hearing her story, you will understand why Courtney's request moved me so.

1/16/2003

To Whom This May Concern:

I'm writing in regard to my present situation. I'm currently residing in Olmsted County Jail. The reason I'm writing this is because I'm a repeat offender. I've enclosed just how extreme my offenses have been. I have about 53 other names which will also be enclosed. These are names that I used when I was a prostitute and traveled to many different states.

I have been in institutions since I was 12 years old. When I was first placed in the institution, I had no clue how to even manage simple hygiene skills and had to be taught. My mom and dad had no clue how to raise kids due to their drinking. If you can believe it, my grandmother and great grandmother were also alcoholics. Let me stop just for a second to tell you, I in no way need anyone to feel sorry for me, I'm just trying to give you a little background, something the police reports don't mention.

To sum it up, I grew up in residential treatment centers and group homes. Eventually, I was turned out by the pimps and was taken to many different states. In a way, they became my institution because they now informed me what to do and how it was to be done. I started using drugs just to cope with the reality of my situation. Sleeping with so many different men. Just to pay someone to pretend to love me was better than the truth.

Finally, I woke up and realized that I just couldn't handle it. I broke away from that lifestyle only to start stealing to afford my drugs and they (drugs) became my institution. They got me up and ran my life until I finally was arrested for theft, and then prison became my institution. It was safe, and it became my norm! I started to have friends, I was functional, I worked every day, and in fact I've worked every department the prison has to offer. I am requested immediately upon my returns, I'm proud of that. I have been told that I have a high IQ, and it only takes someone once to show me something and I'll always remember. In prison in California (I acquired a degree) in Cosmetology, I actually maintained a 4.0 GPA. I have never typed before so please don't judge me on that.

I was released this last July 6, 2002. I had no parole to do, so I had no plan. Even when I have a plan, I always fall on my face. If you were able to see my crimes, you would see how stupid they are. That's what happened this time; I was rearrested on July 15, 2002 (9 days after release from prison) on felony theft.

I have never paid a bill, I have never had an apartment, and I get anxiety just trying to go to the supermarket to buy something. Most people have no idea what I'm saying. I take meds to help but the 10-day supply that prison gives runs out, and there's no money to refill. It's hard for me to find resources. I can do time; I could teach classes on how to do time! Going back to prison would be so easy for me. It would be so safe and familiar. But guess who continues to pay the daily amount of money to house me (which is very high); you people do! Then I lose that little bit of hope that still shines within me, that I think someday I can make it!

There is a program that is just for people like me; it is Teen Challenge with a (high) recovery rate for the most undesirable. The breaking free program in Minneapolis (where donations) are given to help women. I'm 38 years old, and should I even think it's possible at this age to even fantasize that I can be a productive citizen? Have I wasted the life God gave to me? I am a good person with a big heart, I just need a chance. Don't you think? I don't need sympathy or for anyone to think I'm looking for an easy way out, could anything for me be any harder?

XXXXXXX (name)
ADC Detainee
Olmsted County Jail, Rochester MN

This letter, along with her completed application, was approved by our admissions department. I remember the day she entered the program directly out of the Olmsted County Jail. She came in the front door with handcuffs and shackles on her hands and feet. Her only clothing was the orange jumpsuit the county jail had given her while being incarcerated. I just happened to be in the lobby when two Olmsted County Sheriff's Deputies brought her through the door, gave us a copy of the court order, took off her shackles, and left. Those who have visited Teen Challenge know that I have always had my office placed close to the admissions lobby. It reminds me every day of why this ministry is here. People come through our doors very broken!

Over the years, I have seen literally thousands of intakes, and believe me, I have seen some interesting admissions. However, I can't remember ever seeing anyone as excited—even giddy—to be in this program as this woman was that day. The joy on her face brought a smile to everyone. I remember her telling us how happy she was to be out of jail and somewhere safe, even if she had to come all the way to Minneapolis. As our admissions staff looked over the court order, they noticed something unusual. The judge, not knowing the protocols of our program, gave her special permission to leave our facility (once she arrived) to gather necessary clothes and personal hygiene items. Right away our staff tried to talk her out of this, but she assured us all that she would be back. Seeing the gratitude that she had—just to be in our program—we all thought she would be right back.

We waited. And waited. The next morning, regretfully, we called the woman's probation office and notified them that she never returned. Hours later, we received a heartbreaking callback. Probation informed us that this woman would not be coming to our program because she had died of a drug overdose. This bothered me for days. How could this happen to someone who needed this program so badly and was so thrilled to be here? I remember thinking that if we had a women's program in Rochester, we might have avoided this tragedy. As I continued to pray, the stronger I felt that such a program was indeed God's future plan for us.

Now, ten years later, the burden for a women's center in Rochester resurfaced. After Courtney's confrontation in the hallway, the waters began to stir, and the more I prayed, the greater the burden grew. Each time I would run into Courtney, I would assure her that I hadn't forgotten about her request. Over the months, my comments to her transitioned from "I'm still praying!" to "Someday we ARE going to have a women's program in Rochester." She would nod her head hopefully and then go on her way. Looking back now, I believe that the Lord powerfully used both of these women's stories to motivate me! And not just me, but God began to speak to many others about this need as well.

One individual that God had been clearly speaking to was Tom Truszinski, our Rochester center director. A year before my experience with Courtney, Tom was so moved in his heart for this need that, on his own, he had approached the Assisi Heights administration to see if they would ever consider selling some of their land for a potential women's home. The request had hardly come out of his mouth when he heard them say, "Absolutely not." They went on to tell Tom that all the Assisi Heights Convent and property was their heritage and had to be protected for the preservation of their Franciscan Order. They also explained that over the years, many builders and developers had approached them to sell. As a result of these numerous requests, a formal decision had been made by their group to discontinue any additional land sales. It was out of their hands now!

After that conversation, Tom spent an entire year searching for potential sites. From Albert Lea to Winona and throughout all southeastern Minnesota he looked and found nothing. He knew we didn't have any funding for a project like this, but he sensed that God was urging him to keep looking.

It was now a year later, 2015, and we had just opened the new adolescent program in Buffalo, remodeled the dorms in Duluth and expanded our facility in Brainerd. Construction costs had far exceeded our budgets, and we were behind in our capital campaigns. At the July board meeting, it was decided that the Finance Committee would come up with recommendations for these shortfalls. The recommendations were painful: cut one million dollars from our 2016 budget. Needless to say, this was not a good time to consider expansion in Rochester, especially if the community hadn't yet raised anything toward this project.

After the July board meeting, knowing that there were huge budget cuts pending, I purposely tried to refocus my attention away from Rochester. I believe in prudence and responsibility. It is irresponsible to consider expansion when you are talking about major budget cuts like this. It's time to tighten the belt, eliminate unnecessary spending, and focus on effectively managing our 2016 resources. God, however, doesn't always work in the same realm of reality as we do. Sometimes He asks us to follow Him even when it doesn't make sense. This would be the case with the Rochester women's expansion.

During the time when our leadership team was heavily focused on how to cut the budget, Tom received a call from Assisi Heights asking if MNTC was still interested in acquiring property. The nuns had been praying about our request for property and sensed the Holy Spirit prompting them to contact us. They told us their hearts were moved for women in addiction, and that they were willing to make an exception for MNTC and sell us one acre. Knowing that we had looked for years for the right property in the Rochester area and that this was most likely a once in a lifetime opportunity, we continued the dialog.

What will it cost us per acre? And we can't do it with just one acre, will they consider selling us two? Days later, realizing that we couldn't do it with just two acres, we apologetically expanded our request to three. The Sisters then said that they would need to pray about this and get back to us.

Tom wasted no time and contacted our real estate agent, Al Watts. Knowing that MNTC did not have any funds available for a project like this, but since this was such a rare opportunity, we couldn't afford NOT to explore it. Days later, Al came back to us with a market value of $120,000 per acre and $360,000 for the total three acres if the soil was adequate for construction. I knew that this was a valuable piece of real estate but had no idea it was worth over a third of a million dollars—way too much money for us in the midst of major budget cuts. While this appraisal was not encouraging news, I was still interested to hear what the Sisters' asking price would be. I think all of us at MNTC knew that the board would never be open to any discussions of program expansion in Rochester in light of our economic condition. So, when the day came for the Sisters to meet with Tom about their asking price, I didn't even drive down.

Well, that was my mistake, because as the Sisters met with Tom and our real estate agent, God did three incredible miracles. While we were expecting to hear an asking price of about $360,000 to $400,000, the Sisters most unexpectedly said, "We believe in this mission, and we would like to sell this property for the same value that we sold the property 30 years ago to the nursing home," (which is now the current MNTC Men's Home). That amount would be $12,000 an acre or a total of $36,000.

Upon hearing this – and here's the second miracle—Al grabbed his own wallet and said, "$36,000! I will buy it for you."

So, I missed both God encounters. I was sitting in my office without a hope in the world that we would be able to afford a property like this, and here our real estate agent (who we hired to help us) was going to buy it for us.

Upon hearing this – and here's the second miracle — Al grabbed his own wallet and said, "$36,ooo! I will buy it for you."

With the good news, however, also came some bad news. The only property that the Sisters allowed us to purchase was the land that was located immediately east of our men's campus. Unfortunately, most of this area was composed of solid rock and not suitable for construction. When Tom finally shared the good/bad news with our leadership team, we didn't know how to respond. Here our real estate agent was offering to purchase the property for us, but what good is the deal of a lifetime if it is not suitable for construction? After consulting with our architect, it was advised that we bore some soil samples. This is done by drilling small holes into the soil and looking at the rock thickness, type, and density at various spots where construction is done. This process is not cheap, but without these samples we would never know if the property would work for us.

Lynette and I prayerfully decided to pay for the samples ourselves, but before we could even write the check, we were interrupted by miracle number three: a donor stepped forward and covered the cost. We wasted no time in hiring a local drilling company, and to our amazement, the samples revealed that as long as we built above grade, we would not have to do any major rock extraction. This meant that we would have a small, restricted basement area, but this was fine with us. After sharing this news with our architect, we asked him to sketch some rough drawings for a 30-bed facility so we could get estimates on construction costs. He came back to us with a price tag of around three million

---

... before we could even write the check, we were interrupted by miracle number three: a donor stepped forward and covered the cost.

It was now November, and up to this point, other than our board chairman, none of our board members knew anything of the recent developments in Rochester. Because we had been only exploring an opportunity, I didn't feel it wise to bring up the subject of program expansions during another round of budget cuts.

However, after receiving the report concerning the soil samples and knowing that the property would work well for us, it was time for direction from our board. Our full board meets quarterly, but since a smaller group of leadership meets each month, I approached them with the recent events of Rochester. Needless to say, they were amazed. Our development director, Barry, and I showed them the rough drawings of the 30-bed facility that our architect had sketched with the three million estimated construction cost and asked if they would give us a grace period of 30 days to present this opportunity to a handful of donors.

We believed that if a donor stepped forward to help fund this project, then we would know it was the Lord, and if not, that would also be a clear answer. However, we felt that this was a once in a lifetime opportunity and not something we could just walk away from. Once again, we had everything to gain and nothing to lose.

Because there is such a select few of MNTC donors that have the ability to give at this capacity, a lot of prayer went into our meeting. I have to confess that approaching a donor for a multi-million-dollar gift is not easy for me. I become nervous and anxious! There have been many times that I have asked donors to help on major projects and have been turned down. The rejection can be very intimidating–even hurtful. However, whenever I have seen the waters stir and have an assurance in my spirit that this is God's project and not mine, I have a boldness that is not normal for me.

Over the years, I have also seen something very special with many major donors of Christian ministries: they see their calling as a ministry of stewardship. They will tell you that their wealth is not theirs, but God's, and they are *mere facilitators* of the resources that God has given them. What this means to charities asking for help is this: major donors pray first, and then they listen to God. They also want to see the stirring of the water. If they see God at work and God speaks to them, then they will respond. This is exactly what happened in this case.

By the time we were able to set up a handful of meetings with major donors, we were now into December. None of them responded on the spot but did ask for information and told us that they would pray about this and get back to us. It would be up until the week of Christmas before we received a call from a donor and his wife. They let us know that God had spoken to them about this Rochester women's home, and they would be sending in a check to help with the project. They hoped we would be blessed with the amount because they would be sending in three million dollars, the total amount needed to cover the cost of construction. I almost fell out of my chair when I heard him say this.

This meant that (1)miraculously, God gave us property estimated at $360,000 for only $36,000, (2)incredibly, the real estate agent who we had hired to help us negotiate on the purchase price offered to buy it for us, (3)against all odds, the solid rock property that no one was supposed to be able to build on turned out to be the perfect building site, and the crown jewel (4) a donor stepped forward and offered to completely pay for all construction—the three-million-dollar fee. How do you even begin to thank God for such a *walk on water* kind of miracle? Rochester was now going to have a 30 bed women's home!

Our full board meeting was now coming up in January, just weeks after we had received the huge check. I couldn't wait to share the exciting news! Up to this point, less than half of the board knew anything at all about Rochester, and those who had been in on any of the early news still knew nothing about the three-million-dollar check that had come in.

Months earlier, right before we had asked our architect to create some rough drawings for the women's program, our leadership team met to talk about the size and type of program we would develop in Rochester. Because finances were limited, we knew the program had to be small, and thirty seemed to be the right number. We also knew that we could not have a long-term and short-term program together in a building that held only 30 clients; it had to be one or the other. It was unanimous that we start with the short-term licensed program for 30 clients, and then (several years) down the road, we would look at starting a long-term program. This would be our recommendation to the board in January.

About two weeks before the board meeting, one day while praying, I had the most unusual experience. As I was praying about the new women's program, I felt so impressed in my spirit that something was wrong. I reflected back to the day we had decided as a group to go with 30 beds, and I couldn't remember if we had even prayed about that number. I felt very strongly in my spirit that the Holy Spirit was saying, "Not 30 beds, 80 beds." I don't claim to hear from God any more than anyone else who will ask His will. However, I felt so strong about this in my spirit, I asked God to confirm what I was feeling by saying, "If this is of You, then let all the leadership, including the board, be in favor."

At our next meeting, I communicated what I felt the Lord was saying. I think most everyone was positive with the idea.

We decided to go back to our architect and ask for an expansion of his rough drawings to now include dormitory and classroom space for an additional 50 women. He worked on the drawings and came back to us with an estimated additional three million for this expansion. My heart sank as I thought to myself, "Now we are at six million just for the new women's program, and the board wants us to be looking at budget cuts!"

When the day of the full board meeting came, the board spent the first 45 minutes of a two-hour meeting talking about the budget shortfall. God was gracious in that meeting because we had just had a wonderful fourth quarter, and the huge budget cuts that the board had been considering were now unnecessary. The January meeting had a full agenda, and since the subject of Rochester women's program was the last item of discussion, I had only 10 to 15 minutes to present. While I was excited to share the miracles of the Sisters' willingness to sell the property, the real estate agent's offer to purchase the property for us, the soil samples, and lastly, the three-million-dollar check, I honestly was not looking forward to bringing up the subject of 50 additional beds for the long-term program.

As I shared the first part of the miracle, excitement was high. The board was thrilled with what God had done! And when I began to share with them what the Lord had spoken to me about the 50 additional beds and the three million it would take to do this, to my amazement there was not one person in opposition! In fact, it was like throwing lighter fluid on a hot fire. They responded to the vision with a huge "Amen! We can do this!" God's presence was in that boardroom, and everyone could sense it. I've never seen our board so excited about a multi-million-dollar campaign.

> ... it was like throwing lighter fluid on a hot fire. They responded to the vision with a huge "Amen!"

I've heard it said that where God guides, he provides. The three-million-dollar campaign actually turned into a four-million-dollar campaign. In the next 12 months, Barry, Tom, and I were able to raise almost all of these needed funds. At the end of our year-long effort we looked at what the Lord had done. God gave us three acres valued at over $360,000, three million in a construction gift, four million in a capital campaign, and when the building was completed, an individual donated over $200,000 in landscaping, trees and shrubs. This totaled $7,560,000 in less than 15 months during a season when we were facing severe budget cuts. The building was completed and opened in 2017 totally debt free. Today the Rochester campus stands as one of the most beautiful and elegant Teen Challenge properties in the nation, and the women's program remains filled with the *Courtneys* of southern Minnesota.

Major structural damage inside the Tubman building

Removal of all stucco and windows on the Tubman building

18

God Told Me to Call

Women's programming has always been close to the heart of this ministry and its leaders. Shortly after Minnesota Teen Challenge was incorporated, (back in 1982) the board opened their first women's residential program near Summit Avenue in Saint Paul. Regrettably, this program was forced to close down months later due to zoning issues. After I took over MNTC in 1992, and completed work on the Clinton House, my foremost goal was to open a women's facility. Back then, there were very few options for women who needed residential treatment, especially for those in need of long-term programming.

Once the first men's center opened, our phone began ringing off the hook for a women's program. Honestly, the hardest thing in life for me to do is turn someone away who is begging for help, especially women trapped in addiction. But it wasn't long before our dream did come true. We were ecstatic to finally open the Hudson House–our first residential facility for women! It wasn't

a perfect scenario though. While the Hudson House had bedrooms, it lacked program space. We were limited to the top two
floors, and clients and staff soon found themselves tripping over
one another. We needed to find more space, and we needed it
ASAP.

I knew from previous meetings with the City of Minneapolis
that any future expansion of our programs required them to be
made in licensed board and lodge facilities. Unfortunately, these
facilities are a rare find. They are seldom, if ever, on the market,
and they are always listed at exorbitant prices. To complicate
matters, neighborhoods are generally resistant to group homes
moving into their communities—especially facilities that tar-
get those struggling with chronic addictions and past criminal
records. I knew that unless we found another board and lodge for
sale that had been used in a similar manner, grandfathering in our
kind of program, it would be virtually impossible to expand. On
top of this, the City of Minneapolis had a quarter mile distance
restriction requirement between all Minneapolis group homes.
This restriction further limited our options, not to mention the
fact that we had no money to purchase another building anyway.

Looking *in the natural,* our chances of expanding were all
but nil! Remember, back then we were in survival mode, existing
from hand to mouth day after day. Unless God did a miracle there
was little chance that we would be expanding our women's program anytime soon.

But once again, the waters begin to stir. One day unexpectedly, a donor called me up and began to tell me about a building
near our other facilities that was for sale. It was owned by the
Women's Christian Association, another nonprofit that had a

mission similar to ours. The building was a licensed board and lodge facility with a capacity for more than 100 beds. I told him that I was very interested, so he set up a tour with the real estate agent to take a look. While walking through the building located at 1717 Second Avenue South, I noticed several things that concerned me. First, the building was mostly bedrooms. It only had two lounges and a few offices, not nearly meeting programming needs for a drug rehabilitation program serving over 100 people. We were told by the real estate agent that the building was built shortly after the depression to house women who came from the rural areas into Minneapolis to find work. All they needed was a place to sleep and eat; social activities and employment took place elsewhere.

I was in a quandary as to what to do. Our women would be living at the facility for up to a year, and programming would take place at the building all day long. How could we make this work? Well, being in survival mode, the very fact that there was any board and lodge facility available in the city made me think twice about turning this opportunity down. If necessity truly is the mother of invention, then perhaps we could convert a few of the bedrooms into classrooms, and make this program happen.

I asked their real estate agent if we could set up a meeting with the leadership of the charity to share the MNTC mission and our interest in the property. The meeting went very well, and we were able to negotiate an asking price of $600,000, a reduction from what they originally wanted for the building. I let them know that I wasn't committing to anything and that this would all be contingent on the board's approval. I'm so thankful that the subject of financing did not come up. If they had known that we didn't have a dime to spend on this project, I don't think they would have given me audience. While $600,000 is a lot of money now, back then it seemed more like *six million*.

If they had known that we didn't have a dime to spend on this project, I don't think they would have given me audience. While $600,000 is a lot of money now, back then it seemed more like *six million*.

After my tour of the building, I went back to our board of directors and told them about the meeting. I let them know that board and lodge buildings like this are very hard to find, and if we passed this up, we may have to wait a long time before another one might be available. I also let them know that the location was strategic for us. This 1717 Second Ave. property was only 14 blocks away from our main campus. I thank God again for a visionary board. We prayed about this opportunity and felt like the Lord was leading us in this direction. That's when they gave me the green light to approach several donors and see what God might do.

How do you raise $600,000 cash in a matter of weeks when the ministry is surviving day to day and operating hand to mouth? I prayed about this before I set up a handful of meetings with individuals who I thought could help. Needless to say, not everyone was as excited about the project as I was. Disappointment was beginning to set in when God showed up in a special way. I had asked a business owner from northern Minnesota who lived about two hours away to come and look at the building with me. He rarely came down to the Twin Cities. When he made his way through the streets of south Minneapolis and finally parked in front of the 1717 Second Avenue building, he jumped out of his car and began to laugh heartily. He pointed to it and said, "I was always very moved by the needy women who stayed there. My roommate and I used to live in the apartment building across the street and we would watch the ladies come in and out of that building all day long." He then looked at his wife who had joined him for the visit, and with an understanding smirk, they both chuckled.

I am once again amazed that as huge as Minneapolis is, God brought the right donor 30 years later to his old stomping ground to reignite a burden for hurting women. After looking the building over, this donor offered to pay for half of the purchase price! Then just a few days later, two businessmen came to see the project and offered to pay off the rest of the balance! God was pouring out the miracles! In a matter of weeks, we had raised the total amount to purchase the building.

As you might expect, the program immediately began filling up with women. As I shared earlier, the building was never originally set up for a residential program. There were no offices, classrooms, counseling rooms, no chapel, exercise or recreational areas, and there was very limited lounge space. We ended up improvising any way we could. We took all of the bedrooms on the main floor and converted them into offices, a lounge, and

classroom space. Even after these modifications we found ourselves short on program space. Ultimately, to make things work,
we ended up transporting the majority of the women to other
buildings for programming each day. This proved most burden-
some on our staff and clients, especially in Minnesota's extreme
weather conditions. From the very beginning, we had planned
that this would just be a temporary solution until we could either
find another building or do the necessary buildouts on the property. Unfortunately, our wait would take longer than expected.

It has been nearly 20 years since we acquired the 1717 Second
Avenue property. Shortly before the writing of this book, our
women were still living in one building and doing their studies in
another. Over the years, we've added a few additional offices and
lounges, but the building was just never built to handle that many
people. Our staff and clients at 1717 Second Avenue have been
more than gracious. They've watched us expand into Brainerd,
Duluth, Rochester, Buffalo, and the Twin Cities with various new
facilities, and all this time they have patiently waited, hoping that
someday their facility needs would be met. The board, sensing
that the time was long overdue to address the spacing issues in
our women's program, made the decision that this project would
be our next priority. There would be no more expanding the program to other regions of the state until we had first addressed this
long-neglected need.

But where would we begin? We started first by looking at
the option of expanding on the current site. The 1717 building is
located in a densely populated area of the city. Finding on-street
parking is often a nightmare, and all around us are large apartments and multi-family structures. Our architect was telling us
that this expansion would take up our entire courtyard area, and

we would lose almost all of the green space and trees on the lot. To further complicate things, he also informed us that this property was located in a historical district of the city. This meant that any and all renovations would have to be approved by the historical society and be in conformity to all preexisting architecture in the neighborhood. Lastly, this remodeling project was not going to be cheap! Preliminary drawings had the project coming in over five million.

None of our board members were 100 percent comfortable with this scenario, so our leadership team started looking at other options. Relocating the women's program to another site could work. As I mentioned earlier, opening a new drug treatment facility in any decent neighborhood in the Twin Cities is virtually impossible. Even if we could find such a site, the purchase price would be far out of our reach financially. At the end of the day, all roads seemed to lead back to Rome. Remodeling our existing building appeared to be the only viable option, so we started the application process with the city. The first requirement was to get approval of our renovation plans through the Historical Society. After multiple meetings with their leadership over modifications to our building plans, we were now ready to go before the Minneapolis Planning Commission and then on to the City Council for approval.

Have you ever found yourself moving forward on a plan that you didn't feel right about in your spirit? This was how many of us felt about moving forward on this remodel. We sensed that something was wrong, but we couldn't put our finger on it. God's timing is always perfect. He's never in a hurry, and He is never late. We would find this out shortly!

Have you ever found yourself moving
forward on a plan that you didn't feel
right about in your spirit? This was
how many of us felt about moving
forward on this remodel.

We were now in the middle of our application process with
the city when I decided to invite our Minneapolis City Council
representative over for a tour. Not only did we need her support
on the project, but this was a great way for her to become more
familiar with our mission. At the end of the tour, as we were talking
about our women's project, she said, "Are you guys aware that just
half a block down the street, The Tubman Center is moving, and
their building is up for sale." This caught all of us by surprise. We
knew nothing about this.

Everyone who knows this property agrees that the old
Tubman building is prime real estate. It is a 60,000 square foot
facility that sits right next to the overpass on 35W and Lake Street
and is one of the most visible buildings from the interstate. This
property is strategic for commercial development being located
right next to the new transportation hub where thousands of
commuters pass daily. It was also right across the street from the
main south Minneapolis Post Office and directly across the street
from the City's Fifth Police Precinct. It was perfect for developers looking at commercial construction or large high rise housing
units. But it was also highly strategic to MNTC! It borders our

20-apartment staff housing unit and is literally a stone's throw from our main campus on First Avenue. Most importantly, this huge complex had all the necessary board and lodge licenses that MNTC needed, licenses that would be easily grandfathered in for us.

What also excited me was that it would add critically needed parking space for both that building and our nearby facilities. The more I thought about it, the more excited I got! Having a 60,000 square foot women's facility right next to our largest campus would be a huge win for us. Staff and clients could easily commute between buildings. If the building was still on the market, and we could negotiate a fair offer, this option made a lot more sense.

Right away after my meeting with our city council member, I met with the Tubman leadership about their future plans. They confirmed that they would indeed be selling, but also informed me that the building had structural issues. Evidently, the building had not been constructed properly and had major settling inside with some walls dropping more than four to five inches. Also, the windows needed to be replaced along with the stucco. The appraisal for the work was estimated at around 2.5 million dollars. When I told the board that the Tubman property might be available for purchase, they were excited, but instantly they became wary after learning that the building had major structural issues. They were also concerned that the obvious problems might only be the tip of the iceberg. And when they came to find that the purchase price and construction fees were much more than what they were comfortable spending on this project, they decided to step away from this opportunity and continue plans for the build out at our original 1717 building. While this was a bit of a disappointment, I also supported everyone's concerns with the property. If God wanted us to acquire the Tubman building, He would make it clear to all of us.

It was many months after the board made the decision to walk away from the Tubman property when I received a phone call from a pastor who I hadn't spoken with in years. After exchanging our greetings, he went on to explain that recently while he was in prayer, God had spoken to him. He said, "Rich, God said I was to call you and tell you to contact Dick S., and he is supposed to help you." He gave me the phone number, and then told me to reach out to him. I asked him what this was about, but he didn't know the answer. I was just supposed to contact this individual. I immediately Googled Dick's name and found out that he is a founding partner of one of the leading commercial real estate consulting firms in the Midwest. His firm specialized in managing complex design and construction projects on behalf of owners. These skills were exactly what we needed at time, especially after finding out how comprehensive the structural issues were on the Tubman building and what it was going to cost to repair.

"Rich, God said I was to call you . . ."

I called Dick right away and was thrilled with the conversation. It just so happened that he was a serious prayer warrior also, and God had prepared him for my phone call. He began to tell me that just weeks earlier, while he was praying, God told him to immediately go to his cabin and wait for a man that evening who would be on drugs and desperately crying out for help. The Lord then told him that he should help this individual get into MNTC. Sure enough, that same evening a guy showed up at the cabin desperately addicted to meth and crying out for help. Dick was able to help him into our program and was so appreciative of what we do.

When I told Dick about the call I had received from the pastor and about the Tubman building, his spirit was filled with joy. And right then, he offered his services free of charge to help us in any way he could. Only God could prepare such a thing! Because the board had written off the project, we had been at a standstill until God again stirred the waters!

After talking with Dick, I was so encouraged! Maybe our vision for the Tubman building was to become a reality after all. God sent Dick at just the right time to help us evaluate the necessary construction issues and costs associated with Tubman building. Over the next several months, Dick worked with numerous engineers and contractors to pinpoint exactly what needed to be done. With this information, we went back to the board. They were now much more comfortable considering the project knowing that Dick's company had done all the necessary due diligence. The more the board looked at the benefits of purchasing the Tubman building versus remodeling the old 1717 building, their decision became clear. For only slightly more money, we would have just what we needed—all located just half a block away from our main campus.

The bad news, however, was that we would need to raise an additional seven million dollars for the Tubman renovations.

At first, this seemed overwhelming, but the more I put together recent events, the more I could see God's hands all over this: the phone call from the pastor who, through prayer, asked me to call Dick S; at the same time, the Holy Spirit was directing Dick to help the meth addict and interface with our program, and the fact that Dick had exactly the kind of professional expertise we needed to help us locate the problems on the building and generate the estimated repair costs. I have to say again, when God begins to stir the waters, all we need to do is be obedient and jump in. That's when the miracle follows.

After prayerfully considering our next steps, the Lord led us to talk to a businessman who had helped with a number of other expansion projects. At this meeting, the Lord showed up again in a very powerful way. This businessman and his wife were very excited about the project and offered to give us three million dollars. This was just the kind of confirmation needed to move the board forward to secure the building.

We had hardly signed the purchase agreement when weeks later, MNTC was asked to attend a local charity golf event. HOM furniture company hosts a tournament each year, and over the past 15 years has given proceeds of the event to us. At the end of the tournament day, the players are invited to dinner where prizes and awards are presented. This evening went as scheduled, and as planned, the owners presented a check to MNTC and asked me to give an update on the program. As usual I spoke about our growth, the need, and our successes throughout the year. I don't know why, but this year my talk went in a little different direction. I gave the usual update and talked about the need. I also shared about the Tubman opportunity. I knew that the Tubman organization was a charity that was near to everyone's heart and did similar work to ours, so I thought the audience would be thrilled to hear about the transition.

When I finished, I thanked everyone for the generous donation and turned the mic over to one of our graduates who is now our men's director, Terry Francis, who then shared a short testimony. As Terry was speaking, I noticed that the business owner was motioning for his wife to come over to speak to him. She nodded and then sat down. When Terry finished, the owner's wife went to the microphone and said, "Rich, we need you to give us that check back because we have a different amount to give you. Instead of the couple-thousand-dollar check we just gave you, we have a 3.5-million-dollar donation to help with the Tubman purchase and remodel." Because this completely caught me off guard, I lost it.

> "Rich, we need you to give us that check back because we have a different amount to give you. Instead of the couple-thousand-dollar check we just gave you, we have a 3.5-million-dollar donation to help with the Tubman purchase and remodel."

With the tears flowing down my cheeks, the owners of HOM shared how God had spoken to them about helping as I was sharing the need. I would not have expected this to happen in a million years. God had done it again! In just a matter of months, God had given us over 6.5 million dollars to prepare a home for these hurting women. This whole series of events couldn't possibly have been coincidental. No, with masterful timing, He'd hand selected responsive individuals and moved them into place to create this miracle. But what was about to happen next would not only catch us all by surprise, but forever impress upon me the faithfulness of God.

Burned and looted Post Office just 50 feet from our new
women's home

Completely remodeled Freedom Manor
(formerly the Tubman building)

19

Trial By Fire

The miracle golf tournament donation occurred in August 2019, and the following December we closed on the Tubman building and renamed it Freedom Manor. Because it had been used as a battered women's shelter for women and children, their board asked for an additional six months to use the building until school was over and everyone could properly move out. This worked out great for us because it gave us time to raise additional capital before we started the much-needed remodel.

Everything was working like clockwork. That is, until December 31, 2019, when U.S. news media began covering a story coming out of Wuhan, China. A new virus causing pneumonia-like symptoms was headed our way, which some infectious disease physicians were calling the next possible "worldwide pandemic." Sure enough, over the next several months, this disease—now known as the coronavirus—spread across the world like wildfire. As it moved ominously across America, original predictions were for death tolls into the millions. By March, Minnesota businesses, schools, restaurants, churches, and the general population were at near lockdown. While MNTC was allowed to stay open, tight restrictions were put on the program.

Mask wearing and social distancing were required protocols 24 hours a day except when clients were in their rooms. Family visits and passes were discontinued. Not only were those affected by the virus quarantined for two weeks in their rooms, but anyone who came in contact with someone who was positive was also quarantined. Client morale at MNTC plummeted as we watched attendance drop. Frustrated clients had little place to go or things to do and felt imprisoned in their bedrooms for months on end.

Across the state, we watched the virus spread dramatically in facilities where large numbers of people lived under one roof, such as nursing homes and congregate care facilities. On any given day, MNTC has up to 750 clients living together in 13 campuses across the state. As you can imagine, we remained in a heightened state of vigilance. From March to October, we watched hundreds of our staff and clients become infected with the virus. Daily we prayed Psalm 91 over the program, and as far as we know, only a handful were hospitalized, and all recovered well. The rest experienced minimal symptoms, or none at all, even though they had tested positive.

We'd never experienced anything like this before. Generally, my drive into the City of Minneapolis each morning would be four lanes of heavy traffic, full of vehicles kept to a slow 30 mph in a 65-mph zone. During the year-long outbreak, traffic had dwindled down to a mere trickle of cars. Few people were going out of their homes. Every news report was dedicated to following the pandemic trends. As weeks turned into months, I watched people's attitudes change. I watched individuals enter our program with a greater level of hopelessness than ever. It seemed that everyone was becoming weary.

Things came to a head on May 25, 2020, when the George Floyd incident took place near our campus in south Minneapolis, drawing worldwide attention. *USA Today* stated that the resulting riots were the largest civil unrest events in U.S. history, accounting for over 1.4 billion dollars in damages. And alarmingly, the rioting targeted two of the nearest Police stations in the vicinity of George's death. The first large riot targeted the third police precinct where the police station and dozens of nearby businesses were burned to the ground. The next night, rioters targeted the fifth precinct located 50 feet from our Freedom Manor building and immediately adjacent to our 20-apartment staff housing.

Since internet sites that helped direct the rioting were all focusing their attacks against the fifth precinct that evening, we went to the Minneapolis Police begging for protection. To our surprise, we were told that like the night before, the police would be standing down and there would not be any police presence around the rioting that night. They basically said, "You are on your own." We all knew that except for Divine protection from the Lord, our new building would go up in flames just like the dozens of other buildings the night before. We also knew that the rioters might not exempt residential housing units (similar to our buildings) because the night before, a brand new 198-unit affordable housing complex that was sitting empty had been burned to the ground. Our new 60,000 square foot building (under renovation) was also vacant with no fencing or barriers. We would need God to intervene!

> . . . we went to the Minneapolis
> Police begging for protection. To our
> surprise, we were told that like the
> night before, the police would be
> standing down and there would not
> be any police presence around the
> rioting that night. They basically said,
> "You are on your own."

Also, just 30 feet away from Freedom Manor, stands our 20-apartment complex which houses MNTC employees and their families. If the Freedom Manor building burned, so would our staff housing. We knew that just like the night before, due to no police presence, we could not count on the fire department to come. We asked our clients and staff to pray. We also were concerned because just half a block up from the fifth police precinct is another–and our largest—campus. About 120 men were living at this facility, and we were concerned for their safety as well. We quickly moved them to another location for the night, and as we were all running around in a frenzy trying to prepare for the inevitable, unbeknownst to me our women's staff came up with a great idea to make signs to put all around our new building. The signs said things like "Women and Children Live Here," "This is Our Home," "God Bless You," etc. These signs would make national news and ultimately be the deterrent to save our building.

Sure enough, that evening as predicted, crowds into the thousands began to swell in front of the police station and onto the Freedom Manor lawn. Earlier in the day, the police were able to erect a large security fence with concrete barriers around their campus. So, when rioters were unable to penetrate the fence to get at the fifth precinct building, out of frustration they attacked nearby facilities. They looted and burned the post office to the ground just 50 feet from our front door. Across the street was a gas station and strip mall that were all looted and burned. Then they moved on to the Wells Fargo Bank, emptied the ATM and set the entire bank ablaze. From there, rioters hit every commercial building up and down the street for miles.

The only commercial building that remained untouched was our new Freedom Manor building. As I stayed up almost all night watching the coverage of the riots and looting, I noticed multiple reporters commenting on how our building had remained untouched.

As I stayed up almost all night watching the coverage of the riots and looting, I noticed multiple reporters commenting on how our building had remained untouched.

The next morning, I got up at 6:00 a.m. and drove down to the Freedom Manor and Stevens/Hudson campuses. Most of the nearby buildings were still burning. The smoke was so thick that I found it difficult to breathe. However, despite the devastation to the neighborhood, our building stood intact! I noticed the hundreds of graffiti images on all of the buildings around MNTC in every direction, yet I could not find one stroke of graffiti on any of ours. I also noticed that on every storefront and commercial building that wasn't boarded up, windows were shattered, and buildings looted, yet our unoccupied Freedom Manor was left untouched. God had protected us just like He said He would.

A month later, as I looked through a window of Freedom Manor, I saw what was once a beautiful and thriving neighborhood now standing as an empty war zone with burned lots and brick buildings full of graffiti. As I began to question why this all had to happen, the Lord reminded me of the early days with the Clinton House and how He had faithfully turned my discouragement and despair into joy and victory. He spoke to my heart that someday this war-torn neighborhood will be rebuilt with brand new structures and thriving businesses.

As I write this book the neighborhood is transforming daily. The buildings all around us that were once destroyed and looted have been rebuilt with new construction and are now open for business. Our whole neighborhood is being revitalized with plans to make it one of the nicest areas of the city. The miracle of Freedom Manor will stand for years to come as a testimony of His faithfulness in a very dark hour in human history. His Word and His promises are bedrock solid and powerfully alive.

Rich stands next to our new CEO, Tom Truszinski

20

The Purpose of the Stirring

Throughout this book, I have reflected on many incredible and miraculous things God has done with buildings, properties, and programs. It would be greatly remiss, however, to bypass the *why* of it all. It all comes back to the Bible passage that opened this book:

In these lay a great multitude of sick people, blind, lame, paralyzed, waiting for the moving of the water. (John 5:3)

I'm persuaded that the Angel of the Lord didn't swirl the waters of that pool merely to console hurting people with the idea that there is a faraway God somewhere, detached from human misery, and that someday, we could *perhaps* find a comfort in the afterlife only. NO! That courier angel was sent with God's own signature—the power and demonstration of the Holy Spirit. He would create a stir such that, if a person responded in faith—believing—a miracle would take place. It would be a transformation impossible by human means alone. It would be God-breathed.

The buildings and properties and programs that have been assembled at MNTC are a necessary precursor and truly God-inspired foundation, but they are only that. They've been set in place to house the eternal work–the passion and heartbeat of God Himself–the souls and lives of mankind.

As it was 2000 years ago, so it is today: all around us are multitudes of emotionally, psychologically, and spiritually infirmed folks. Even as I write this book, drug and alcohol abuse is at an all-time high. Our cities are filled with increased crime, violence, neglect, mistrust, and despair. Nationally we are experiencing a mental health crisis, with people living in increased depression, fear and anxiety. Suicide rates are at record levels despite the fact that we have the greatest dependence on psychotropic medications in our nation's history. I see hopelessness written on the faces of those walking through the doors of Teen Challenge almost every day. They themselves will be the first to tell you that they don't just need another program—they need a miracle.

While programs are very important, they often times fall far short of solving society's woes. I believe the best answer for change in human behavior comes with a change of the human heart, and no one does a better job of transforming the human condition than God Himself. Saint Augustine in 400 A.D., said it best when he wrote, "Thou hast made us for thyself, O Lord, and our heart is restless until it finds its rest in thee." Augustine understood that the human heart needs to trust in a power far greater than ourselves. We will continue to be restless and weary until this relationship with God is restored.

Through my years of experience, I have developed a deep respect for the 12-steps of Alcoholics Anonymous, which are considered the most widely used and accepted method in the world for acquiring sobriety. The first step is foundational: (1) we must admit that we are powerless over this addiction. From there come the next two critical steps: (2) we must believe that there is a power greater than ourselves; (3) make the decision to turn our wills and lives over to Him.

Almost my entire career has been devoted to helping people overcome addiction. And in my experience, without the implementation of these first three steps, I don't see a lot of successful recovery. Whether we call them "steps" or principles, or just plain old repentance, there is a reason why these 12 steps have become so popular: they work! Biblical spirituality is interwoven throughout all 12 of these principles or steps.

Miracles happen and lives change when we intertwine God and a repentant heart, just as the steps teach us. We have seen this kind of miracle take place in the lives of those who enter these doors, time after time. As far back as I can remember, I've kept my office located near the admissions lobby, allowing me to witness the most chronic, desperate and hopeless individuals walk through these doors, only to begin the process of transformation just days later.

As a Christian, I believe our loving heavenly Father is continually at work drawing us back to Himself. Whenever we respond, He does the same. James 4:8 states, "Draw near to God and He will draw near to you." When God draws near to us, and we respond, relationship begins. Christianity is really all about us responding to that stirring.

Our graduates continually tell us that, while they appreciate the contents of the program, the real lasting transformation they encountered here came when they responded to the stirring of God's Holy Spirit in their hearts. I believe this is the number one reason why we see success. Over the past 30 years, there have been multiple outcome studies done on our program. Each time the results have revealed that Minnesota Adult and Teen Challenge has some of the highest success rates in the country. While we can attribute some of this to talented staff and great programming, beyond a doubt—without the work of God's Holy Spirit moving in hearts—our outcomes would look meager at best.

Over the years, we have seen tens of thousands of lives impacted by this program… so many miraculous stories that I wouldn't just need a few extra chapters, I would need hundreds of volumes of books. Someday maybe that can be my next project! Honestly, I can hardly go anywhere across this state—in a mall, a park, a church, a gas station, nearly anywhere— that I don't find someone coming up to me to say, "Do you remember me? My life changed at Minnesota Teen Challenge." They tell stories of coming from utter hopelessness and despair, but now living lives of joy, blessings, and complete fulfillment. In more cases than not, while visiting, I can sense that the stirring of God is alive in them still. That relationship with God they found here at Teen Challenge didn't stop after leaving the program.

The 12 steps end with what I believe is one of the most important keys to our sobriety. That is, once embracing the challenge and having had a spiritual awakening, we will commit to carrying this message of hope to others. Nothing is more encouraging to me than when I run across our graduates, and they share their testimonies of helping others find hope. I believe this is a key component to sobriety; we have to give out to others if we want to receive it ourselves.

My challenge now is to you, the reader. Around all of us are paralyzed, blind, lame and sick co-workers, neighbors, family and friends—individuals we know personally who would give anything to find real hope. My challenge is for you to ask God to stir your heart in a special way. And then, as you trust God's voice, pray for His guidance, and step into the water, the Father's tender-hearted compassion will grow within you—a compassion to help others, perhaps even thousands—as He has done at Minnesota Adult and Teen Challenge.

Acknowledgments

From the very start, God met the needs of MNTC through the faithful gifts and volunteerism of His people. It has never worn off for me—the amazement at how He answers our prayers by sending the right help at the right time. Nowhere is this stirring seen more evidently than in the lives of our volunteers and donors who help keep the doors of this program open. As their waters are stirred, they give out to others, and in turn, God gives back to them. Their waters become life-giving fountains.

We are utterly dependent on you, our donors and volunteers, to keep these doors open. Tens of thousands of God's people have stood with us over the years to make this ministry happen. How can I and this entire organization say 'thank you' adequately? Your sacrifice at times has literally moved me to tears!

I especially want to acknowledge two businesses that have been our greatest supporters: Wayne and Char Johansen, co-owners of HOM Furniture and the leadership of Sea Foam Sales Company. These organizations have faithfully stood with MNTC for decades, and most of our strategic growth has been a direct result of their support. They have not only sacrificially given of their resources but have invested hours into our residents and staff. God has used them in incredible ways, and we are totally indebted to them.

Next, I want to acknowledge all of our staff, senior leadership and Board of Directors. And special thanks goes to board members who have gone the extra mile like John Roise who faithfully served over 20 years, Chuck Beske, Bill Bojan and Jay Coughlan, board chairs who have all given extraordinarily of their time and energy to make this organization what it is today. Special thanks and honor go to board member Pastor Mike Smith who has faithfully served on this board for just shy of 40 years now. One of the original founders, he has also served on the Executive Committee of the board that meets every month. He also hardly misses a Saturday visiting one of our centers ministering to our residents. Without his support, I do not believe this organization would have survived.

I want to give special mention to our President Eric Vagle. Eric works full-time for Teen Challenge and manages all the operations and administration. In the 30 years of working together, I have never ceased to be amazed at his giftedness and most importantly, how he walks in integrity and respect. He has been my right-hand helper and endeavors to make me look good.

I am highly grateful to Pati McConeghey and my wife Lynette for their work in editing the manuscripts of this book.

Lastly, special thanks for my two daughters Holly and Robyn and my wife Lynette. They have always been at my side, willing to help in any capacity needed. Even though times were very difficult in Africa, and the early years of Teen Challenge were very demanding on our family, they have always been the Lord's inspiration to me, cheering me on and celebrating the victories together.

MNTC Timeline

1990	Scherber Family returns from Africa
1991	Rich agrees to take over MNTC
1993	The Clinton House opens
1995	The Hudson House opens
1997	The Steven's staff housing opens
1998	The Nicollet Avenue property acquired
1999	The Portland House opens
2000	1717 2nd Avenue Women's Home opens
2003	The Steven's Square Nursing Home purchased
2006	Duluth TC and Grace Manor open
2007	Hope Commons (former Mt. Sinai Hospital) acquired
2008	Brainerd TC is opened & Petters fraud exposed
2013	Rochester Men's facility acquired
2014	Lakeside Teen Boy's property acquired
2017	Rochester Women's program opens
2019	Tubman building acquired
2020	George Floyd riots
2021	Alexandria TC launched
2022	Rich passes CEO baton to Tom Truszinski and a new chapter begins

About the Author

Rich Scherber is the CEO of Minnesota Adult and Teen Challenge, one of Minnesota's largest chemical dependency treatment providers. With 13 campuses across the state, and an average daily enrollment of 850 clients, they provide outpatient, inpatient, long-term residential and extensive aftercare services. In addition, they provide the largest drug prevention program in the state, presenting to more than 60,000 adolescents annually.

Rich grew up in Rogers, Minnesota. He has earned a BA Degree from Northwestern University in Washington and a Master of Science in Psychology from the University of Wisconsin.

In his teens and early twenties, he struggled with chemical dependency. After finding sobriety, he entered the ministry where he has been active for the past 47 years. He spent five years working as a foreign missionary in South Africa during the Apartheid before he was asked to take over the leadership of Minnesota Adult and Teen Challenge. At that time, the organization was on the verge of bankruptcy. Since becoming CEO 30 years ago, the organization has grown to 13 campuses across the state serving an average 850 clients daily. Newsweek Magazine has twice listed MNTC as one of the top ten treatment providers in the state.

Adult & Teen Challenge
Minnesota

Get help now. Call 612-FREEDOM | Visit mntc.org
Minnesota Adult & Teen Challenge currently offers the following programs throughout Minnesota

For adult women and men:

> Licensed Treatment for Substance Use Disorder
>> *Residential (up to 90 days)*
>> *Outpatient, Telehealth*
>> *Special tracks: opiates, pregnant women*

> Residential Recovery Program (about 12 months)
>> *Residential faith-based program*
>> *Special tracks: veterans; moms with active child protective services cases*

> Licensed mental health services
>> *Substance use disorder, co-occurring mental health, general mental health*

> Transitional housing for graduates of our Recovery program

> Leadership training for graduates of our Recovery program (1 year program – Minneapolis)

> Aftercare services

For adolescent males (age 14-17 years) – Lakeside Academy

> Faith-based program

> Behavioral health (anger management, character development, integrity)

> Licensed treatment for substance use disorder

> Licensed co-occurring and other mental health services

> On-site public school and vocational training

Campus locations:

> Men's programs: Minneapolis, Brainerd, Duluth, Rochester

> Women's programs: Minneapolis, Rochester

> Lakeside Academy: Buffalo, Minnesota

> Adult outpatient and virtual services: offered statewide

Adult & Teen Challenge
Minnesota

For information or to make a donation, call 612-FREEDOM or
reach us at MNTC.org

Minnesota Adult and Teen Challenge
740 E. 24th St.
Minneapolis, MN. 55404

To order additional copies of this book,
call 612-FREEDOM and ask for the Development Department
or email: Development@mntc.org